Whisper

By

Lou J Free

Printed in USA

ISBN 1-893075-44-3
Library of Congress Control Number: 2002103024

Cover Art by Sharon Dale Thurston
Graphic Design by Tim Dickey
Author Photograph by
Bob Parker Photography Studio

Portland, Oregon 97232
www.spiritpress.net
publisher@spiritpress.net

Acknowledgements

Thanks for opening doors through your work

and being.

Spiritual love has touched many because of you.

Shirley MacLaine

John Edward

This book is dedicated to

Alma Elizabeth Haile Garner

Osborn Ignitia Garner II

Foreword

"Lou J Free wrote this how-to book for you to honor your angels and put the 'natural' into the supernatural. This is important because as you begin to unfold expanded awareness, it's nice to have some step-by-step encouraging words. Otherwise, it's a little like going on a road trip without a map."

Lou J interweaves fascinating real life stories and examples with clear explanations of the rules of the road. You are not alone.

A vast and glorious world of departed loved ones and guiding spirits are eager to take you by the hand. Lou J Free may be your earth angel who whispers to you through the words and wisdom of this book.

Sit back relax and have a great read — bliss awaits.

Shelley Stockwell, Ph.D.
co-author of
The Search For Cosmic Consciousness:
The Hypnosis Book Einstein Would Have Loved

Angels Whisper

Listen in stillness…hear what they say…

Angel whispers reveal the miracles in your life…

Messages from the other side to this side

Listening

The words are hushed. They are like whispers to your soul.

Angels speak whenever we listen. They don't yell and they don't insist. They give us gentle messages, but they are the most powerful force of communication you will ever have. Angels and guides are the connecting energy to the dimension beyond our life experience here on the earth level. We spend most of our time thinking and wondering why we are here and what our purpose is. As human beings it is an inherent search, unexplainable, but always a part of us. Never doubt the reason for our being here is to return to pure love.

We have come to learn and return.

Our souls are a part of a universal energy, meaning our thoughts and actions contribute to the whole of it. The more love we accept, the more love we have to offer, forming the cycle we came to earth to experience. Experience is what we get when we don't get what we want. When we don't listen — experience and consequences become the teachers. Calling it an experience rather than failure has a more positive tone, which helps you move on more quickly rather than dwelling on the results. Don't get stuck!

I believe we repeat the incarnations until we learn

what we came to learn. We can go to "school" as long as we choose…this life or the next or the next. We will do it until we get it right. Those claiming to be old souls are probably just the slow learners. We have free will choices at every point. We consent to come back into a particular setting, choosing the time period, gender, our families, the lessons and even, I believe, our astrological patterns. Your astrological chart was laid out at the moment of your birth. It is based on the time, the place and the date of your birth. Your astrological sun sign designates and reinforces your abilities and talents virtually creating a map of your time on earth.

The tools and situations we choose depend on the missions we are returning to complete. We are given the strongest circumstances and the best tools to learn as quickly as we want. Those from the other side, our guides, our teachers and our angels, surround us. They are always accessible if we call for help or need guidance. We only have to ask and then listen.

Listening seems to be the most difficult thing for human beings to do…listen and truly hear. We all have a tendency to say aloud, "Let God's will be done," but finish the sentence by adding "as long as I get it by six o'clock today.". In my observation every earth being has one major lesson in common — patience.

Patience is the conscious decision you
will stand still until the right action occurs.

We are constantly being shown by signs all around us, but rather than listening and hearing what the right action is we become a little arrogant. We decide we know best, we know how to make it work, or we think we can fix it. Surrendering, allowing, and letting go frightens us since we think we are in control. The big lesson is we never have control.

We have no control. We have free will to change our perception, to react differently and to accept the occurrence.

As human beings we may become very focused on the earthbound happenings, tending to analyze everything rather than accept it. We have a propensity to prove what has happened rather than recognize the message. We get caught up in figuring it out. Our "reasoning sense" sometimes overrides our "intuitive sense". We think we have control over our lives if we are able to manipulate what is going on. This is life's biggest illusion. Certain events are inevitable. Our free will grants us the choice of how we will deal with them. In our logical and analytical approach our interpretation can easily be misconstrued or excused away. We find ourselves caught in the same cycle of stagnation, repeating the same blueprint and paying a high price for the rut we are in.

Ignoring the signs simply prolongs the lessons. By continuing the situation the circumstances will get progressively worse until we are forced to make the change. Being forced to make the change at this point gives you little choice. The difficulty in making the change creates the stress, which could have been avoided. If the message is to leave the relationship and we want to hang on, we will find a way to justify staying in the dead-end, abusive and stagnant situation.

Have you ever heard this before: He will get a divorce as soon as the kids are grown…then out of college…then married…then after the grandkids come? This is not a time for patience. The "dead-end" signs were there from the start and the choice to ignore the warnings caused a lifetime of hurt and waiting. This lesson will come around again with the same ending unless there is a change in the behavior. It could be the same partner or a different one…it doesn't matter since it is an individual decision having nothing to do with the other person. If you are complaining to your friends about the state of affairs and are only mentioning the other person you aren't getting it. Discuss the relationship and use only your name. Are you able to still talk? When you have to say "I" you have to admit you are allowing and perpetuating what is happening. This could be an eye opener. The message is to halt the course of action.

Another "trying to fix it" justification: He said he was so sorry for hitting me and he brought me flowers and he said he would never do it again. He probably has a running account at the florist. We have so much hope this time that it will be different. We think we can fix it by trying again and again. The hook is when they say, "You know I'm trying."

Trying is lying. "I'm trying" means
"can I talk you out of making changes?"

Or another scenario: She swears she will stop spending the grocery money for drugs, and she will take care of her babies. She promises she will be different. She will make a home for the family. Trying doesn't count. Doing is crucial.

Choose what you will allow in your life without
justifying, explaining or defending your
life decision. Be steadfast. We call it J-E-D.
Don't Justify, Explain or Defend.

Waiting for it to get better or hoping we can fix it causes us to detour from our path. Remember, it is a detour. We must always return to the path no matter how many detours we take. This is how we wind up in dilemmas, which are hard to recover from. We have lost valuable learning time. The destination remains the same. We can choose how long it takes to get there and the baggage we will carry with us. Change is frightening to most of us. We would rather keep repeating our learned behavior; at least the pain is familiar.

We wonder if we should give them another chance and yet another chance. Maybe, we reason, "My kid will get a job, and get out of the house, if I just allow a little more time." After all, twenty isn't very old. Have you ever seen the forty-year-old still at home letting someone else take the responsibility for his or her life? Well, they were the twenty-year-old not that many years ago. You make your decision, then they must make a choice. The amazing thing is both parties grow and have a new self-respect when boundaries are drawn. We can give up the struggle with the "baggage." Make the journey without it.

When no one draws boundaries
everyone becomes bound — growth stops.

Job situations can be an area of real difficulty since we spend most of our waking hours centered on the interaction with others. I have seen groups living out the same pattern in a work-team they went through in their past lives. The scenarios can range from recreating a harmonious team-effort in building a skyscraper to reliving a fight-to-the-finish competition in a hockey game. It is a replay.

If we live past, present and future lives simultaneously we are dealing with the past and future in this present moment. When we recognize and remember the past, our course in learning becomes easier. If someone in a past life stole your fortunes of gold in Egypt you may get a really good price for gold coins from an Egyptian in this lifetime bringing a balance and a closure. Many people who came in to be the spiritual example may become the millionaire living the lifestyle while maintaining ethics and higher moral behavior. It could be a reward from their past life. Everyone has an individual experience. Those working in the grind of an industrial company may wonder why they are stuck in a place with such negative energy. They are teachers. They may be the only positive energy on the job site. They teach, and they are truly teaching through their illustration of being a spiritual person. They are not being chastised or punished. It is <u>not</u> a karmic debt. Some return to be earth angels and guides in human form.

As human beings we can more easily accept messages when we hear it through human words. Then we begin to acknowledge their whispers. They are teaching us to listen through verbal messages, which might not be seen as an intuitive "hit" otherwise. It is easier to dismiss or misinterpret if we think we aren't psychic. Our logic says it can't be real.

Intuitive messages may come through human words to validate what you have already sensed, felt, heard or seen from the other dimension.

We are learning the information is real and is there for our higher good. Our free will choice is to follow through. Our choice could be to just ignore the messages and we must then take responsibility of the consequences.

When we stop repeating the same pattern, we set a new precedent. Listening and making better choices means we are evolving. The change creates a new attitude. We only change ourselves. We never change others. The change in our actions forces those around us to react differently. An entirely different living situation then develops.

When we choose to stop listening to someone complain about their job over and over again the energy changes. If they are only interested in complaining and finding a "dumping ground" for their problems they will find someone else to listen. When you stop listening they may understand they need to change jobs or their attitude or at least not complain to you. You draw a boundary. You stop an energy draining interaction.

Everyone in our life has free will choice to accept or reject our new behavior by respecting it, or they move out of our lives. This is true growth. You will know it and feel it when you have stepped through the door. Your life will suddenly expand when you unblock all the possibilities offered to you. You have opened the door bringing a new rush of excitement and anticipation with it. You are alive in your life.

Many never recognize the responsibility is theirs to make it work. They continually beat their head against the wall, in the same place over the same things. They will complain they are living the same undesired existence, day in day out, without realizing they set it up. They haven't recognized the only growth comes through their focusing on what is best for them. They have to consciously choose to allow only energy inspiring people and situations to be in their life. Your test is to find out your part in the development.

Is taking responsibility and learning to follow through, my lesson?

Am I completing unfinished business from prior lives?

Am I to be the example of a higher spiritual consciousness?

Is my behavior creating desired results? How did I set it up? How did I allow it to develop?

We become the student...walking the walk not just talking about it.

The whispers tell you. Our guides and angels are there to steer us without interfering. Why are we always learning, only to be tested over and over? We are learning to trust. Our major emotions narrow down to these basics…fear and love. We yearn for acceptance, approval and love. Fear can immobilize us. If we have expectations that aren't met, we become disappointed. Our tactics can then become fear based. We begin to analyze. What should we have done…what if…why? *Anticipation* without *expectation* is important to understand. There is a difference. *Anticipate* and plan your day, but accept your day as it unfolds. Expecting it to occur only as planned results in disappointment when it varies. *Expectations* unfilled may seem to be a failure. There is no disappointment if there is *anticipation* without *expectations*.

We are protected. It may not feel that way at the time, and we may whine about it, but to realize it is for our higher good stops the fear. We must look for where the experience has placed us. We may have been put in the precise position for our miracle, the miracle of new awareness.

When we came to "earth school" we separated from pure love. The pure state of perfection is what we remember on a soul level. We remain a part of the universal energy, but the completion piece is now missing. From our first earthly breath our desire is for the missing piece. Searching outside our self begins the greatest effort to reconnect. Our soul searches for love.

We look for it from everyone…our parents, those around us and our mates. Our lesson is to learn to love ourselves. In reality, searching for love may be why we try so hard to find love through a mate. Our most intense search may come from our personal and intimate relationships. When we come close to finding unconditional love, we know we have encountered a soulmate. We are *remembering* the wholeness.

Each soulmate link expands our progression whether the relationship is with parents, friends, acquaintances or the love of our life. We re-create the situation we had in our prior life in order to learn the lesson. Through conscious awareness we relive the similarity.

For instance, if you were a nurse on the battlefield of *World War I,* you might be the school nurse in this life. If you were a knight in shining armor in the other life you might make protective gear for policemen. You duplicate the pattern, but change the scenario. The lesson is learned and you won't repeat it with anyone; the karma is finished.

You are evolving with each step moving to another lesson and another level. This is your celebration, growing closer to a harmonious life, remembering the state of love.

Those who have near-death experiences revisit *the place* of perfect love. This is why they are very reluctant to come back into the earthbound body. If they have lessons or life purposes remaining they have to come back for completion. They may have karma to finish for being unkind, or they may come back to be of help to a loved one. There are individual reasons they return, but strangely everyone's story is the same…they would rather be there. They usually come back kicking and fighting, wanting to stay in that beautiful place. They describe the beautiful place, the joy felt, the loved ones seen there and the brilliance of love. Their guides and angels may be seen in crystal like settings of clouds. Most travel through the tunnel of white light.

If they had remained, going through the physical death, they would transcend and be born again, picking up where they left off in the learning process. The lesson to be accomplished would be the same. If you took advantage of people in another life, you would become the "victim" in this life whether you were originally stealing in ancient Rome or robbing in the 1800s in England, the lesson would be the same. Again, all the choices are ours and the balance of the universe must come to pass.

At these times our angels and guides are there to help as we make our decisions. Our life profits by the information we hear making our purpose and our path become clearer and clearer. We have a "light bulb" moment, which turns into a "runway light" as we become more and more sensitive to the significance of the messages.

It took time and practice before I grasped the magnitude of this lesson. I had learned the law of acceptance. I learned patience. I learned to anticipate without holding an expectation. It sounds like the same thing, but it is quite different. Anticipation means I plan, manifest, hope and pray for what I want. My mantra is "make it right for me and the universe." I can ask for all I want as long as I am not asking at the expense of others. I must not expect it to happen. If I have expectations I am not allowing. I accept what comes — trusting it is bringing me the experience I need.

Acceptance means what is meant to be
is received as an opportunity to grow.

Messages come in so many ways. If they don't believe in the possibility, people tend to dismiss the information. Others accept it in total confidence they are getting help from those on the other side. It is recognizing that as energy we simply go beyond the physical realm to another dimension. Those in that dimension don't have to deal with the physical, earthbound problems so they are available to be a more objective observer of what is happening. They don't judge us. They don't interfere.

Psychic ability develops by being open, void of ego,
with pure intent to pass on information.

The stronger my intuition grew the more I became the switchboard to the other side. To hear, I listen with a different part of my senses to the impressions they offer. The message might be called telepathic. The whispers come through all my conscious senses as hearing, seeing, smelling, tasting, touching, and going beyond these senses. It has, I believe, been appropriately called the sixth sense. I found an interesting connection in Glynis McCants' book, *Glynis Has Your Number*, with the number six, the vibration of the home and nurturing. Glynis writes, "The six house is a house of beauty and warmth and a magnet for children." The number vibration affirms our sense of wanting "to go home." I found it interesting that an inverted 6 is a 9. Nine Glynis notes is "a house of the humanitarian — all are welcome." Every sign I recognize bears out the absolute correlation, which runs parallel to everything in the universe.

Everything in existence is connected. You simply have to be aware to recognize the patterns. You have to accept you are a part of the energy and you affect the universe and all that is around you by your actions and thoughts — be they positive or negative. The message is "what you put out, you get back" "what goes around comes around," and — to paraphrase Job 4:8 in the Bible "You reap what you sow."

The sixth sense is the means of communicating to the other dimension. The messages could be described as a knowing. It comes in waves of signals and signs. You could equate it to tuning in a radio dial, adjusting and seeking the frequency until you can understand the meaning of what is being said. Messages will find a way to get to you.

A movement out of the corner of your eye is the energy of a guide or entity letting you know they are there. A question, which has been running through your mind, is answered by a song with meaningful words. Finding a coin or a feather in an unusual place is a signal for you to pay attention.

We are developing our other sense, a sense to receive these messages through a different frequency, which is hard to explain. With practice it is a sense we can learn to use as often as a thought goes through our head. I often wonder how we came to know and name our five senses. I feel certain God didn't put a limit on them. Did we just stop exploring? Did we assume this was all?

I wonder if the seventy to eighty percent of our brain matter, which we've been told we don't use, is in actuality blank tapes we haven't developed. Could it be stored information from our past lives? All possibilities must be left open. The talents and genius qualities people demonstrate at unusually young ages maybe stored memory. The child who plays concertos with no teaching is difficult to explain. They haven't been trained or taught or shown how to paint a masterpiece or write prose or sing opera, but they can do it.

There was a time not long ago when hypnotism was unheard of. Many thought it was an evil spell. In modern day healing hypnotism is used successful in altering brain waves to reprogram the subconscious. The unknown is always frightening to the masses while it is exciting to those who are eager to explore. I am convinced our being exposed to the sixth sense and psychic phenomenon through the news media and entertainment field is to educate the masses. We become familiar with the concept. Then, we can imagine the possibilities. Movies, television programs and books document actual incidents people have gone through forcing us to consider the probability there is something beyond what we see. There seems to be proof. When proof is set before us we instantly look for a logical explanation. Those who are bound and determined not to acknowledge the proof dismiss it with "it is unexplainable" as though this ends the discussion. Being unexplainable does not mean it isn't real. The messages are real with explicit details.

Messages Are Gifts

The capacity to bring messages from the other side is truly a gift. Many people struggle with the psychic capability as though it were a burden, but with some training and understanding it will be recognized as a blessing. In the Bible it is written in First Corinthians chapters twelve through fourteen about the gifts and how they are to be used. I believe it is a God-given ability, and I fully believe He would not offer us anything, but a blessed gift. The messages must be brought with a loving intent.

Inevitably during a reading someone will ask, "How did you know that?"

"I don't have a clue," is my answer, "if I concentrated on how and why I wouldn't have time to hear the messages." It is about getting out of the way, and listening. This is what everyone needs to learn. Everyone is psychic. It is like singing — everyone can sing. Some are naturals. They sing in the spotlight without training or lessons, and everyone wants to hear them; others become a success after studying and training with practice, practice, and more practice. Some people need to stick to singing in the shower; they sound wonderful in the shower. It may be in a shower, but they can sing. The ability is there for everyone to develop.

Using your psychic sense every minute, awake or in your dream state, is what you strive for. Practice increases the power.

Be curious and open. Always start by consciously protecting yourself with your prayer, mantra or a ceremony. Create your own method or ritual by combining some of these:

Light a candle. Most people use white, but each color has a purpose and a meaning.

Smudge. Use sage, cinnamon or any other item you choose.

Repeat a chant or prayer verbatim or spontaneously.

Visualize protection. See mirrors, white light, a bubble, surrounding you and the area.

Ring chimes or bells in sequence or randomly.

Place crystals in a protective pattern.

You will feel the right ceremony as you experiment with these and more, remembering the point is to spiritually bring only light and love into your space. This should become a natural process you develop into a habit. Learn to do any of these rituals in your visual consciousness whether you have the tools or not. Your aura, your physical body and your spirit will respond, changing the energy around you. Learning to live in this space keeps you ready for information from the other side to come through to you. You will be in the right place, at the right time and in the situation you were meant to be in.

Staying in a constant state of awareness allows signals to come to you with ease.

In the time before a reading I become prayerful and still. It is as though I am fine-tuning the connection. I breathe deeply hearing the breath. I bring in protection as I ask for the guides and angels who have information to gather. I ask they give me any message someone needs to hear. This is fast moving. I begin to hear, feel, sense and see words, scenes, and pictures. Smells occur.

I prepare to bring the messages, meaning I shift into a different space. I have to leave the ego part, which thinks or judges or becomes logical on another level. I have to simply be the conduit, the message bearer or the relay. The ego can be so fearful of being wrong that the message is blocked. The other extreme of a reader being egotistical is believing no one else could possibly be as good. Either condition causes misinterpretation or judgment of the messages. Passing the information on in a tactful way is both ethical and spiritual.

A psychic, medium or reader is only the receiver not the originator, just the facilitator.

Create Your Ceremony

Create Your Mantra and Prayer

Why Do We Get Information?

We get messages when the message is ready to be received, when we are ready to hear. I have found when a specific question is asked and there is no response from the other side, the answer might interfere with free will. Certain steps are necessary, specific decisions concluded or a change in action has to happen before more information can come through. When no answer comes, and action is necessary, we usually find ourself repeating the same lesson — we aren't getting it so we are in the vicious cycle of no movement. We recognize we are doing it again without knowing how we set it up or how to get off the merry-go-round, which may not seem merry at all. We are repeating past and present life experiences and we are weary of the cycle. Listen and observe. We begin to see we have set no boundaries so the boundaries are repeated. We learn "right action."

We don't have to revisit all our past lives to learn from them. It is the same notion when the student is ready the instructor will appear. Will we be ready to study? We graduate from one level to move to the next. We are readying for the next test. How do we know if we passed the test? We won't repeat the dysfunctional behavior of the past. We know we are growing when we see our life getting better with each turn. We are finishing our homework, passing the test and getting ready for the next phase.

Know God won't bring you an experience you can't handle... a valuable realization.

In a reading I have said, "You will get a new job promotion." They immediately begin to argue with all the possibilities... I don't have a degree... someone else is in line for it... I don't have enough experience... I'd have to move... all excuses.

The energy to block everything has been set in motion. They deny themselves the rewards. The possibility only comes by letting go of the fear. Fear will keep you from making a decision; the only bad decision is indecision. Let go of the doubt. Believe you deserve the abundance of a happy life. Then the new job can develop. Believe you deserve abundance in all things. Trust you are ready. Letting go really means trusting.

Decide... follow through...be ready to make another decision. Find your path.

Accepting the abundance as a blessing removes the blocks. Give thanks and appreciate your gifts. Be patient with yourself and others. Patience means standing still until you know it is the right action. You will know it is right action because your entire being will tell you. You will sense it and your gut feeling will tell you. Be in total awareness, observe, and listen.

List signs, synchronicisties and unexplained happenings

Your Notes of Awareness

List gifts you let pass you by

They Speak Softly

Before doing a reading I begin to listen. I shift into a meditative state even though I may be doing routine earthbound things like making the bed or putting away laundry. The session may be a few hours away when I begin to tap into the other dimension. It feels as though I amble through space announcing we are on our way, so "get the information ready" — get the right messengers there and tell us how and where to be. I stay in a prayerful space. I ask for protection repeating my prayer "only that of light and love" be present. I visualize white light surrounding the entire area from our level upward.

When getting ready for a session I call it "tuning in." In shifting my consciousness you could compare it to the state of daydreaming. You literally shift the brain wave. In this space you are not concerned with the physical; you are functioning, but it is a reflex. You are on another level opening up to any communication, which is meant to come through. I visualize it like a big computer bank of information in the sky with all the knowledge of the universe accessible on a "need to know" basis. We just need the right keyboard, know how to put in the questions and have a good receiver screen. We can then bridge the dimension into other worlds.

Being a curious Leo with a Gemini moon and the duality of a Libra ascendant, I want to examine every concept. I open all my senses. I use all the tools…astrology, numerology, cards, pictures, and articles…whatever opens the intuitive channel for messages.

Using the birthdate symbols from the persons chart helps me focus in on him or her. The astrological birth chart shows the placement of the planets at the moment of their physical birth. If you had looked to the sky above you, the moment you were born, you would have seen the pattern of the heavens that makes up your chart. The chart holds the energy of where the planets and asteroids were the day of your birth so messages and time frames map out your life path. A certified astrologer can trace your ancestry, your past lives and soulmates using the scientific technique. The astrologer reads the placement of houses, degrees and aspects, which allows them to examine your past, present, and future. I use the chart like a psychometry object rather than through the science as astrologers do. Psychometry is reading information from the energy of the chart. It creates the roadmap guiding your life. Having a personal chart prepared is good for a lifetime and a good tool for creating your life.

Many cultures create the chart at the moment of birth as preparation for the life course. The information gathered from it is endless. Most people keep their charts with them like you would your driver's licenses or your passport since most consultants in the metaphysical field use astrology to some degree.

Psychometry is the technique of gathering details from objects. Objects hold the energy of the person, people around them and even what is going on in their daily lives. Some people bring articles belonging to another person they want to ask about. If their intent is loving, and done for the right reason, information will come through them. They in turn pass on the messages. There have been instances where no message came through. The person has to get the reading one-on-one. The lesson may be they must ask for the reading themselves, they have to help themselves.

The messages are, at times, words I see written out as though they were done in skywriting on dark blue clouds. I will see the word in my "mind's eye." I can actually count the number of letters; however, it is curious how often I can't distinguish the middle letters. I can see the first letters and the last letters, but there are those in the center I can't make out. I have tried to use my peripheral psychic vision to read it, but so far this hasn't worked. The visual messages are, in fact, written out in our own alphabet making me think that if I spoke French they would probably spell it out for me in English. They have no limits on the other side.

Next, the movie may come. The visual images can be amazing. They show me their physical looks, how they passed, whom they are with and what is going on. They will explain the connection to you. They can quickly go from the age at which they passed to another time in their life. I have the sense they go back to the best times of their life on earth. They seem to have the gift of choosing their time and setting. You see their favorite outfit at an age during happy days. They may show their physical condition at the end of their life and shift quickly to the healthy, physical body they want to return to. We have laughed to see he was bald at the end and now has his full head of hair back. "Oh, yes," they say, "he was proud of his hair and didn't like losing it."

Those who were crippled were kicking up their heels, smiling and dancing. People with clouded minds are clear thinking now.

I have seen those who suffered extreme physical disease in a healing place on the other side. They seem to be suspended, and as I look, they always appear upward and to the right side. They appeared to be in a type of hospital bed, all white, safe and quiet, as they rested before going on to another level.

When a loved one doesn't come through there can be many reasons they aren't communicating. In their transition, they may have become vividly aware of their errors and mistakes. The hurt they inflicted, the mistreatment of others, human or animal, or abusing himself or herself could be the compensation they are attending to. They must acknowledge the responsibility they have in "making it right," even from the other side. The apologies they extend to those left behind so many times allow the healing to begin and the pain to diminish. Those on the other side move to a different level.

There are those who immediately begin their work of helping us. They seem to leave the physical body easily making their transition to the light by simply walking through the veil. They are the souls who are with us during their passing. They are out of the physical realm, seeing all that is going on during their last breath, the ordeal of burial and the time of mourning. This is when we sense they are watching us; they are. Numerous stories are told of loved ones who have died and were seen prior to their passing in a dream vision.

The dying person may ask if you "can see them?" Those who come to help them cross over stand by. The dying person sees them clearly as they wait. Many at the bedside have watched the dying person follow an obvious energy around the room, even at times talking to them and laughing with them. Those who can attune to this realm may psychically recognize them. There can be a burst of physical energy to their failing body during this time. The dying person may rally. They may seem stronger or more mentally alert. There seems to be a rush of energy when the transition from the physical form to the spirit body happens. Maybe it is the power of the guides and angels at work.

Near the time of passing even though the physical body is still functioning the spirit may be out of the body and appear to others. Those visits prepare us or get our attention. They contact strangers giving information for various reasons, sometimes to solve problems or give answers.

They may come in a wide-awake vision with others seeing their image. Often it happens in a lucid dream. They appear as a farewell visit. Maybe it prepares us in a slight way, but at the moment of death we are never really ready. This is the human part of us.

List any unexplainable happenings connected to a death

List any premonitions

Spirit In Two Worlds

Our angels may be there to help us when a death is unexplainable with no apparent purpose or reason. The most astounding appearance of a spirit trying to communicate came in an unsuspected way. This was a stranger seeking a way to get a message through.

I had booked Lisa to do readings for the weekend. She was on her way to her Dallas office from the Austin office. It was routine trip for her. It was always a fun time with people coming and going throughout the day, getting readings and visiting. The restaurant staff welcomed the group.

I walked into the banquet room of the restaurant where we would be working. I noticed a strange, unrecognizable odor in the room. I wondered what it could be, but dismissed the thought as we began to get busy with clients. Lisa arrived and began to set up in the room. The first appointment started. Mid morning Lisa called me aside and quietly said, "There is an entity in this room. It is just hanging up in the corner. It isn't negative; it is just there. I'll bless it and clear the room later with some holy water."

The readings continued. I again noticed the odor becoming stronger in the room, but I didn't say anything to anyone. It was a damp, wet, muddy smell and didn't seem associated with the restaurant. I was puzzled. I wondered if others had noticed it.

The day went smoothly with one client calling to cancel and when the five o'clock appointment didn't show up we had dinner early. I asked Lisa if she had noticed the very unpleasant odor in the room. She agreed it smelled like something wet and moldy. She had no idea where it was coming from. Maybe we could use some candles in the room tomorrow.

Our first client was waiting when we arrived the next morning. I entered the room to turn on the lights and was overwhelmed by the damp smell. I was hesitant as I asked the owner if she knew what it might be. She said she had noticed it on Saturday, too, but couldn't locate where it was coming from. It was a sunny Texas day so the air conditioning was running non-stop. The air was being filtered, but it didn't seem to be in the ductwork. It wasn't coming from the other rooms. It wasn't being drawn in from the outside. I thought maybe a room deodorizer could help since the odor was stronger than ever. I then decided a spray would have no affect. The staff searched for the source. They found nothing outside the room and couldn't determine what was causing it. They were embarrassed about the smell. We continued with the full day of appointments.

It was late afternoon when I was shocked to see a detective, one of the police force and a Texas Ranger entering the front door. They needed some information and were asking questions.

They showed me a name and asked if she had come for an appointment yesterday. "No." I answered, "She scheduled one in the afternoon, but never showed up." This had been a new client, whom I didn't know. Friends knew she had made the appointment. They knew she was having difficulty in the relationship and needed help. He didn't have a job and had a drinking problem. It was becoming more abusive. What caused her not to show up? She hadn't kept the appointment and hadn't called to cancel. I had no information from the appointment sheet. I asked if there was a problem. I wasn't ready for what he said. The Ranger said she was dead. She had disappeared shortly after five o'clock Sunday morning when she arrived at work to open the store. A fisherman had found her body in the lake, which surrounded the town.

I suggested they bring any of her personal belongings in and we would see what information could be picked up from it. The officers brought her handbag, which had been left in the store. They had her last reports and accounting sheets filled out at work from the day before. They agreed to wait until we had finished with the last client. They were open to any help they could get. A murder in this lakefront town was shocking.

We finished the last reading and told the officers we could go with them to the scene. Holding the woman's handbag gave impressions of harsh words, demanding threats and an altercation. The woman had disappeared from the convenience store at the beginning of the early morning shift. Lisa wanted to feel the energy around her workplace, since being in the area of the crime would transmit more details.

The authorities revealed nothing at this point. We drove across the bridge to the convenience store situated on the bluff above the lake. She "saw" the woman in a confrontation with two men at the store shortly after she opened for business that morning. Circling the building in the van, Lisa stated firmly, "She didn't die here."

We returned to the highway driving slowly toward the area where she was found. Lisa said, “The woman drowned.” We were driving toward one of the many parks and boat launch areas along the seventeen-mile lake lined with a maze of coves. Lisa was certain they had taken this route, and felt two men had put her into a dark colored pickup at the convenience store. She gave a description of the men. They stopped along the way at a house, maybe, but left quickly driving on to the isolated area of the lake. They had parked above the boat ramp. The authorities assumed they carried her down the rock steps to the water. Lisa assured them she was carried down the boat ramp where she was dumped into the water. They dropped something, Lisa insisted. She was confused about what it was. She knew they dropped something as they walked down the ramp. She felt another vehicle was parked across the way, not connected to them, but parked there earlier.

She indicated their truck had been parked near a concrete curb. The officers walked about, searching the ground and found a non-filtered cigarette butt where the door would have opened. The cigarette was not a popular brand so that had been a telltale item to find.

At this point the Texas Ranger said a martial arts type of throat hold probably strangled the woman. Lisa insisted the injury did not kill her, but rendered her unconscious. She had drowned. The officers later explained the item dropped was her glasses.

There was evidence of a confrontation in the convenience store. In the early morning hours, surprised customers found the store completely empty with rolls of change strewn about the floor. It didn’t seem to be a robbery, with little else disturbed around the store.

The other vehicle Lisa had seen parked belonged to an early morning fishermen who had put his boat in at the ramp. He was already out on the lake before they had arrived to dispose of her body. However, someone had broken a window of his truck. Was there a connection? They didn't find one. No one questioned who smoked the brand of cigarette found. Tire tracks of the truck weren't compared since there were other markings in the area. Was that all the information we would get?

When we psychically bring information in to help in cases like these we would love to just see a movie of the sequences as they happened. It feels very frustrating when it comes in bits and pieces. We have to remember we are human beings working in a spiritual realm. We must remain patient and remember…if it isn't coming through, the message could interfere with free will. I feel there are times when no more messages come until we make choices or take certain steps or change a course of action. As soon as those moves are made information comes. If we knew the outcome we might not go through the process. The process can be what we needed to learn. The timing is up to us. We can't question the lessons or the experience.

We have to trust everything happens,
as it should. It is the necessary path.

We gave all the help we could in the case. With the information also came the sense no one would be caught or pay the price for her murder, but this was not revealed to the investigators. This message could have caused interference in the job the law enforcement had to do. They might have been less intense in their investigation. Everyone had a part in this experience. Each had their own responsibility for their actions. I was curious. How did this play out in a past life? What part did we play and which lessons weren't completed?

The three officers were grateful for the information thanking us for the help. They took many notes, but since the investigation was just beginning, they gave us very few details. The autopsy revealed she had, indeed, drowned. The killers thought she was dead, but the water in the lungs indicated she was alive when they dumped her into the lake. They hadn't counted on her body being found so quickly.

The murder jolted this small resort town nestled on the lake just outside the metroplex area of Fort Worth and Dallas. Rumors were everywhere. It was frightening regardless. The town was in shock. They didn't understand how this type of crime could have happened in this close-knit community. The talk was of the strange circumstances. Was this a killer ready to strike another place of business? Was this someone with whom she had issues? Fear and apprehension ran high. The most dramatic emotion centered on those who had witnessed what we now realized was the dead woman's spirit appearing, in the form of the strong odor in the room.

Paranormal events were not something most of them had ever before dealt with. Believing we have souls and we go to heaven with the angels when we die was within their realm. Seeing ghosts, apparitions or entities was not one of their experiences until now. Having a woman's spirit appear before she passed and remain until she was confident the police would investigate, pushed their belief system into a whole new consciousness. Their life would never be the same. Acknowledging there was an out-of-the-ordinary happening, unexplainable but real, forced them to accept there is life past the physical.

This had been a weekend full of insightful experiences. Everyone was contemplative as we parted. Saying goodbye to the officers we drove back to the restaurant to let them know what had happened. The staff and the owner were discussing the ordeal and drawing some conclusions. One person in the group knew of the woman's situation and her circumstances so the suppositions ran wild. It was a shock for our town.

All at once it hit me like a jolt…the damp, muddy type smell I had noticed at the lakeside was the exact same odor I had smelled in the meeting room. Lisa agreed. Since the restaurant was closed the air conditioning had been turned off. There should have been an extreme odor in the room by now. I said, "I have to go check out the room."

I opened the door to the closed room, now quiet and dark, and was stunned. The damp, musty smell was completely gone. I walked around the room; there was no odor…the room was clean and clear. The energy was different. The others joined me and were as astonished as I. The odor was apparently the smell of her body when it was pulled from the water, muddy, damp and decaying. We were stunned at what we were finding…the entity had been present for two days. Now it was gone.

Even though she was in her physical body until Sunday morning until just past five o'clock, her spirit had come to us on Saturday morning. Lisa had seen the entity in the corner and had planned to use holy water to send it away. She never did. It wasn't time for her spirit to leave. Her spirit remained in the room until the police came and left Sunday afternoon. It was as though she led the authorities to us.

The woman's spirit was seeking us out, going ahead of her physical body since she needed help. If her spirit knew she wasn't going to live, did her soul lead the police to us? Did she subconsciously know she was passing while totally unaware on a conscious level? Did she want the officers to learn from us in order to bring justice for her murder? Did she realize no one would be caught and she wanted everyone to know who was responsible? If she were out of her body before her physical body died did people around recognize a difference in her? I know what happened to us that day. I believe she showed us how her life was taken and why.

The vision I had was she knew the two men who came in wanting money, not robbing the store but wanting money from her. She refused. She was not a shy, retiring person; I felt she "got in their face." I felt she followed them out to their truck escalating the altercation. One man, because of his training, had the ability to kill a person by applied pressure to the proper point in the neck. Believing she was dead when she collapsed they decided to dump her in the lake thinking she wouldn't be found.

I could not prove what happened during her death because even the police never had enough to prove a case. I do have total proof through numerous witnesses the odor of her murdered body stayed for two full days in a room where we were. They knew the odor had totally disappeared within one hour of our leaving with the law enforcement officers. What were we to learn? I could only pray she was aware we had done all we could do, and most importantly, that she is at peace. It was more confirmation for me.

Our spirit and soul are not confined
to the physical vehicle... the body.

We can astral travel. We can explore through dreams. We can do remote viewing. Others could actually recognize us when we visit them through spirit. And, we can see and communicate with those without physical bodies.

Many reunite with those who had gone before them such as their loved ones, friends, acquaintances and even their pets, who appear as a welcoming committee. In their remaining days you will often hear them calling out to those who are there to greet them. Cherish the experience of being there when they ask you if you can see their relatives, friends and spouses who have gone before them. And don't forget the animals and pets they loved who were with them on earth will lead them across. You will see their eyes light up and the smile on their face. The reunion is happening. Their passing is a unique journey known only to them. Each passing is different. When I get messages from those who have passed I feel privileged to be the recipient. It is as though I had been invited to visit and each visit has a special blessing.

List those you sense surround you from the other side

"That's My Grandmother"

Larry's grandmother wasted no time in coming through. He sat in the back of the meeting room. He had arrived late having a last minute emergency patient at the hospital. Eva Inez was probably saving a chair for her favorite grandson.

The first sight of his grandmother was of a very ill woman who seemed to be in her late eighties, bedridden, pale and weary. I could see her legs caused her a lot of pain. She showed me slippers she wore and Larry said, "Yes, she had some like that."

It felt as if she gave me this brief glimpse so Larry would know for sure she was there. Very quickly she was back in her early forties showing me a picture of herself in a red dancing dress wearing a broad brimmed hat that matched, tilted to be a little sassy. This was a lady who loved to socialize and it better include dancing. It was as though she were inviting me to her house as I began to see her neighborhood; I was describing the porch, the living room and where the bedrooms were. It was a warm and loving place with lots of people in and out, and no one was quiet. It was noisy with chatter and laughter, and his grandmother barked out lots of instructions, which you had better listen to. Her name came through, Eva. She wanted

Larry to know she was healthy and happy now, and had her dancing shoes on. Then the fragrance of hot, homemade bread came floating through making my mouth water. Larry said, "That was Miz' Mann next door who baked the bread and the smell filled the whole neighborhood."

Larry smiled. I watched the warm memories flood through him. I thanked Larry for letting me visit his family each time she came through, and she usually came through every time he was there. There were many visits from his grandmother during our gatherings and at times she was just visiting. Her first time was to make sure we knew she was there. After this she brought advice to Larry about his trips to Germany and a change around his job and suggestions about his love life. His readings were to guide his life.

She was very talkative and Larry laughingly said, "That's my grandmother." I saw pictures and trinkets and many of the things she loved including her favorite outfits. As I described what I was seeing, Larry easily recognized the information. There was nothing shy or hesitant about her telling us what she wanted us to hear. She sent a message to Larry's niece about taking care of her health. She was watching over her kids and taking good care of them. She was staying close. She was out of her physical pain; she was happy and active on the other side. I always welcomed Larry's grandmother coming through…I love the freshly baked bread smell. She visits often.

Knowing your loved ones are at peace is reassurance we live on through other dimensions. God told us He went to prepare many mansions. I feel the mansions may be the different levels and areas we go to when we leave the physical world. For all of us to be given the assurance that they — and we — live on gives us a different view of dying. It is an acceptance of a far-reaching passage…the concept you move to another echelon of eternal life.

The energy of life exists outside of the physical body and we will learn to function in many dimensions at the same time. We are coming closer to understanding astral travel, out-of-body trips and remote viewing. We are gaining life path knowledge. Our teachers are there to offer new material to us when we are ready to move ahead. All of the opportunities are waiting.

Awareness comes in every form.

We owe much to one teacher, Shirley MacLaine, for opening the doors to explorations into the unknown realms. Her books explained experiences never before written about. The movie *Out On A Limb* was an extraordinary account of guides driving trucks down steep mountains, the colors of auras around us, out-of-body experiences, and floating on the silver cord mentioned in the Bible.

Shirley MacLaine was brave when she brought forth these exciting revelations, and even braver when she talked about what had happened to her. Even today, when I watch her movie, I gain new insights. She was "out on a limb" of an "out of the ordinary" tree baring enigmatic fruit. She shook the belief system of many and excited the rest. And I'm thankful for her bravery in opening doors with her absolute and intense faith. Shirley MacLaine proved psychic predictions were made and came true. She made the connection to her past lives and how they framed this life. And, she talked to the other side through her personal medium, Kevin Ryerson. He was called a channel, which is what we all do when we know things, unexplainably, just know things. She showed us the unthinkable and unbelievable weren't just possible, but were realities.

Another thought provoking movie showed a beautiful love story encompassing this world and the next. The movie *Ghost* depicted the expanse of the universe, showing you could be here and there simultaneously. He was with her when she needed him, helping her on the physical level, and being with her in spirit. When she was strong enough to begin to live again he was able to ascend to the light, staying in spirit with her.

He wasn't earthbound. He could be here and there. He struggled to contact her, but as hard as he tried, she couldn't comprehend the messages. A part of her sensed he was there but the possibility they could communicate seemed remote to her. The part of the medium, played by Whoopi Goldberg, gave in to his unrelenting pleas allowing him to use her as the channel. He used her physical body as a receiver. The medium became the instrument, the spiritual message machine. When the message came through in human words she could believe he was truly there. Because the details were so specific the messages could no longer be denied.

When we agree to be a medium we open ourselves to whomever out there wants to get a message through. We know the importance of protecting ourselves. We have the power to refuse to let an entity come through we feel is negative or objectionable. Just as you saw in *Ghost*, when the room filled with spirits eager to speak through the medium she was like the big X on the heliport pad where they could "land." Those on the other side will seek out a way to get through when they are not being acknowledged.

Blinking lights, turning on the radio or hiding your car keys are a few ways of getting attention. Or they will come through a psychic medium. I laughingly have said God works in strange ways through "strange" people at times when someone needs to hear the message. This is our purpose for being able to communicate with the other side.

Is this really possible? Can we truly talk to another dimension? When we shift to the psychic level we are like a beacon. We become the vortex of energy they can use as a path for communication.

I had to practice shifting into the space allowing the messages to come in. I learned to listen, then repeat, not interpret or judge what I receive. Getting information from the other side has been a development, which began when I was very young, the times when I would just know things I shouldn't have known. I didn't talk about it. I was confused by it, but all the while assuming everyone experienced the same thing. It was a one-way communication in the very beginning. They whispered to me.

Developing your psychic sense is a process led by angels, whether earthly or heavenly.

List your angels earthly and heavenly

Teachers and Guides

I was an inquisitive kid reading everything I could get my hands as soon as I learned to read. There was never enough to read. I even read my dad's Quarter Horse Journals. I dreaded summer vacation since I wouldn't have the school library to escape into. I hated being sick and having to stay home; I missed the chance to find out about new things. I wanted to take in as many undiscovered things as possible, anything new was exciting.

I loved to listen to the conversations in front of the fireplace in the evenings, when the adults were debating and discussing the world situations and what was going on around us. I didn't get to comment or ask questions, but I got to listen all the while forming opinions about what I heard. I always wished I could have joined the conversation. The most learning times were with my grandparents when we settled down on their front porch in the cool summer evenings with no one else around. They discussed everything, and more importantly, they answered my questions. When the questions had impossible answers they discussed "what could be." They talked about the spiritual part of us. Even though we went to church and studied the Bible their beliefs came from outside of the organized religious thinking. I remember the anticipation of hearing stories of what the Bible revealed. Then there were the stories of unexplainable happenings they had witnessed during their lifetime, and the Bible talked about these things. These stories would have been labeled psychic phenomenon in today's language. I never got enough. I wanted to hear more. I could have listened forever. I asked lots of questions.

My grandmother, Mama Garner, taught me the most. She talked about the spiritual world and her visions. She and I talked and talked. She was not labeled "psychic," no one thought she was strange, and she didn't preach. We just knew when Mama Garner made a suggestion of what to do or more importantly what <u>not</u> to do, you had better listen. We just decided she was really, really smart.

My grandfather listened with an understanding of how the future could be foreseen and why. We called him Daddy Babe, his nickname from being the baby, in part, but more so because his name was Osborn Ignitia Garner II, too long and too complicated. He was a tall, strapping man soft spoken with a ready laugh. Mama Garner would giggle and always laugh at his stories even when he would get the endings mixed up because he had told them so many times. His comeback of, "Who's telling this story anyway?" made us all laugh. And, he told those stories over and over with all their versions and they always captivated us.

I was very young when I began Sunday School classes, but I learned the most about religion and beliefs from them. Talking about spirits, ghosts, guides and angels made me more curious than ever. I read the Bible trying to find more parts about the gift of prophesy. My grandparents said these gifts were to be used in a spiritual way as stated in First Corinthians chapter 14. I read and reread the verses trying to understand it all. The more I read the more evidence I found that showed messages were there to help us. These were gifts.

I knew Mama Garner had a special gift. She wasn't like anyone else in the family. And, she didn't talk to anyone else in the family the way she talked to me. I knew there was a special bond with my maternal grandparents especially Mama Garner. The soul connection even showed up in our astrological charts. It showed the purpose and reason they were in my life. I was certain my grandparents were here as my guides on earth.

Mama Garner was wise with strong common sense. I believe common sense is our sixth sense, which everyone has. Some people never recognize it, most ignore it, and some develop it totally. We knew to listen to Mama Garner because too many times if you didn't heed her forewarnings you would wind up in a struggle. She didn't tell you twice and she didn't have an "I told you so" when you didn't listen. In fact, she would giggle at the predicament you would usually wind up in by making the foolish decision.

Mama Garner's sense of humor lifted your spirits no matter what was going on. There was a peaceful acceptance about her. It was as though she knew life would come to pass in a certain sequence and our free will would be the way we dealt with our experiences. She could sense the lesson you were learning and give you encouragement to remain on course. The outcome was obvious to her. She was using common sense to perceive conclusions.

Everyone has psychic capability;
our talking drowns out the whispers.

When messages come through, people tend to become very analytical. They let the logical part of their thinking dismiss the meaning. They choose to ignore the significance. They have selective hearing and comprehension. Mama Garner taught me there was total freedom to choose, but the consequences were yours alone. Repeating the same unworkable situations time after time after time is the consequences. Learn the lesson so you can evolve.

To change the dysfunctional pattern
you must change the behavior.

Mama Garner didn't seem to view your state of affairs as mistakes, but the experience you needed at the time. I now recognize this is the example of a nonjudgmental attitude. She had a gentle way of guiding.

I would have gladly lived with my grandparents. I didn't relate well to my parents or their attitudes. When I could stay with my grandparents I stayed as often and as long as I could. Mama Garner and my mother were very different in their view of life; daughters don't always mimic their mothers. I never felt as though I understood my mother's thinking. Being with my grandparents felt as if I were home. I was blessed that only several miles separated the ranches where we lived in the heart of Texas. I begged to go often. There was a certain peace and safety when I was with them, but the most important element was the learning. The discussions always began with my inquisitive searching bringing a real excitement to my young brain. It was no accident I picked them as grandparents. My life decision, the soul choice, was made before coming in.

The greatest memories were the evenings we sat on their front porch. The kitchen smells of supper still floated through the house as we settled down on the porch swings. The rolling hills were blanketed in wild flowers, which moved in the breeze. Often we watched the deer as they grazed beside the lake below the house. The white tail doe wandered across the field with her twin fawns. She was special since she had twin babies year after year. I remember hearing the quail calling as their sounds echoed through the mesquite trees at sunset. It was God's landscaping, Mama Garner told me as Daddy Babe would chuckle and began another story. I never wanted it to end. I absorbed every word they told me. They expanded my world. They stimulated my thinking in a million directions so I had a million new questions when I went for the next visit.

Our conversations were far reaching. Many of my young questions were the wonderings of what was here in the beginning. What was here when there was nothing? I can remember trying to comprehend nothing — no earth, no stars, no air, no sky — not even a thought. I would lie under a star filled sky and wonder. My mind couldn't get to the place of when there was nothing.

I wondered what heaven was like. Did we come from out there? Did we go back there? Maybe we ascend into heaven as Jesus did. I wanted to know about Jesus. Could he really heal people by laying His hands on them? Where were we before we were born? What happens when we die? Why did babies die and where did they go? Why do some people live a long time, others just a brief lifetime? Could people in heaven hear and see us? I remembered the big picture of the beautiful angel walking with the two small children Mama Garner had hanging near the fireplace. I decided heaven must look like the picture.

I was full of questions. They were patient in exploring ideas and beliefs. They stirred viewpoints with their thought-provoking answers. They encouraged my curiosity. There was never any doubt about the spiritual space they were in. Every conclusion stemmed from the positive belief in the existence of a higher power. There was no doubt our souls are forever. Our consciousness was somewhere before we were born so when we leave the physical body the energy still exists.

I understood the possibility the memories and knowledge from the past or the future would show up in each lifetime through our cellular memory. By using our intuitive sense we can connect to those specific details. This is why we feel a strange familiarity with a first time acquaintance. We have never met them before, but we feel as though we've known them forever. We might look at them thinking "I've seen you before" knowing you hadn't physically met the person in this lifetime. As you become acquainted with them you begin to discover amazing synchronicities. You both love the smell of leather, have puppies named Bingo or you both have unexplained scars on your ankle. If you explore further, through a past life reading, you could find the reason you are together again. You may come back just to say "hello, again" or finish the confrontation you struggled with or maybe you are together this life for a close and loving relationship.

I call this reward time when you come back to reconnect in harmony with few conflicts. There will be a divine purpose with each connection. It is revealed to us when we are ready. Then, through our free will, we can process the experience as quickly or as slowly as we want. I have found many "old souls" who repeat and repeat and repeat their episodes. We will do it until we get it. This is evolution. What is the lesson. Listen and observe. It will become clear.

The soul seeks peace and the search is for love.

The earth path is a journey to learn. We have guides, guardians and teachers to bring God's intent to us. I have found they can be many or few. Your angels and guides come depending on what your need is. I feel they come and go depending on the lesson you are dealing with. Some guides are shared — they help many people while others remain only with you. I can remember very early in my life, probably about four years old, feeling as though I had a lucky star over my right shoulder close enough for me to touch. I recognize now it was my guide and my guardian angel. I remember the whispers, but at the time it was only to let me know they were there.

Visions and dreams are clear messages.

In remembering, I realized my first psychic impression happened as I started first grade. Our collie dog, named Shep, disappeared from the ranch. We were heartsick. Shep was close to being human. He could almost talk; he definitely could communicate in his own way what he was trying to tell you. He had a way of curling his mouth as his whole body wagged making it look as though he were smiling, in his dog way, at us. He had protected us many times. His barking made us notice things we might have missed. Shep would chase away the wolves or coyotes to protect the baby goats and lambs in the pastures. He barked wildly to scare away hawks diving to steal baby chickens. He grabbed snakes and shook them furiously to keep them away. His barking sent many warnings to us. When we couldn't find him we were frantic. We had to find him.

As days went by we were losing hope. Maybe he had tangled with a wolf or a bobcat. We didn't want to think about that. Maybe someone had picked him up. On the fifth night my mother and I both dreamed the same dream. Shep was alive. We saw him coming home walking very slowly around our lake. He was limping and his coat was tattered with tangles and mud. Shep looked very weak, but he was coming home. Our dreams were synchronized messages.

In the morning we awoke and instantly told what we had seen in the dream. Our hopes were high again. Everyone renewed the search, combing the entire ranch, the roads, the creeks, the pastures and the riverbanks. We called his name as we went, hoping to hear his barking. There was no trace. We were so sad, but kept hoping.

On the sixth morning we were ecstatic. We were so happy. Shep was lying on the back porch. Our dreams had been prophetic. He was weak, tired, and muddy. He had a broken leg, but he was alive. He couldn't wag his tail, but he tried. It seemed his whole body was wagging and his eyes were sparkling with happiness. He was glad to be home. We hugged, fed and praised him. We remembered the dream and wondered how we got the message.

We found by further searching what probably happened on the riverbanks. It looked as though Shep had been on the bridge when a car struck him knocking him over the rail and onto the embankment. Where he landed was muddy and so slick he couldn't climb out. There were markings of where he had crawled and how he had clawed trying to climb the embankment. His injured leg and the slippery bank were too much for him. Shep was too far down the river for his barks to be heard. He had tried. He had barked so much he had laryngitis; it was days before his regular bark returned. We set his leg and did everything to speed his healing. We know God gave him strength to survive. If he hadn't have been close to the river to get water he would have surely died.

Shep was alive and healing, and we were remembering the details we had seen in our individual dreams. We called them dreams, but this was different. These were messages, which came from another realm. We both had identical dreams. The details we witnessed of Shep's return are remembered as easily today as then. Shep will surely be there to greet us when we get to heaven. And, I'm sure he will be there smiling and wagging all over showing us he loves us.

When I told Mama Garner about the dream and for the first time she began to tell me of her visions. I was awestruck when she told me about becoming pregnant and waking up the next morning to tell Daddy Babe their third baby was on the way and it would be a boy. She had had a wide-awake vision, not a dream. Mama Garner had seen Daddy Babe holding a baby boy high over his head in his right hand. It was as though Daddy Babe were holding the baby upward to heaven in a celebration of his being born. She knew the vision was prophetic. She saw the angels hovering nearby.

Eight months and about twenty days or so later the baby boy was born. I was amazed and more questions began to form about her other experiences

I loved hearing about her visions. I wanted to hear about every message she had ever had. I wanted to hear all about what she saw. How did she see and hear the angels.

She told me about little Lorrie who was about four years old. She was a beautiful and delicate child, but was frail and sickly. Mama Garner had a vision of her one day. She saw her standing quietly out in a field on a sunny day. There were many angels hovering all around her and over her head. Mama Garner knew little Lorrie was going to pass. She told Daddy Babe she felt as though Lorrie wasn't going to live. These were the early days of the 1900s so communication was difficult between ranches. They were awakened around midnight a few weeks later by the sound of a horse and buggy coming across the river bridge toward their house. She arose, lighted the kerosene lamp and whispered to Daddy Babe, "They are coming to tell us little Lorrie died."

Mama Garner talked more about dying. It was probably in preparation for the passing of a close relative in the days ahead.

Transitions
Birth and Death

My first remembrance of a passing was seeing Ava as she lay dying of a malignancy, which had invaded her hip. No one had ever talked about any feelings or beliefs or the dying process in my own home. It seemed right that Mama Garner was there when I first witnessed death. Being very young, I didn't understand a lot of what was happening, but I felt the concern as they placed her in her bed so she could die at home.

Those in the room were calm as they tried to make her comfortable. There was little they could do for the excruciating pain she was suffering. I remember her tiredness. I remember how pale she was. I remember the resignation in her weak voice as she told those around her to make certain they got their checkups and took better care of themselves. She had worked very hard in her few years in a beauty salon leaving little time for herself. The fear was she had exposed herself to chemicals in the dyes and bleaches, which had caused the breakdown of her immune system allowing the disease to affect her. In working so hard she had in so many ways ignored her physical health in her busy life.

She was ready to end the pain of her illness. She was ready to die. Everyone talked to her, as they stayed close by her bedside. As I look back now, I realize Mama Garner knew everyone had to let go, allowing her to pass. There was an acceptance and peacefulness in the room.

It reminded me of the death scene in the book *Little Women*. As the loved ones gathered around the death bed and watched a mist rose from the body drifting toward heaven. Could they have been watching the soul ascend? I believe so. Instead of watching their death could we actually be watching their birth into the next life? The transition is opening the next door.

Celebrating our birth into the next dimension could be as important as the birth celebration onto earth. Being earth-born means we have come to learn and experience. Going through the birth process entails pain. Birthing requires healing on the mother's part while it marks the beginning life for the infant. The baby comes in crying. The baby has left a warm, safe, and nurturing place where it feels loved and protected into a whole new world of growing and learning. The passageway onto earth removes the baby from this protected state and in doing so, it creates exposure to all the pains, lessons and trials of living in a physical body. And yet, we celebrate the life process of being born.

The mystery of death leaves us in an unknown realm, which creates fear and a lack of understanding when the body is left behind. Dying is not a subject discussed easily even with those whose job it is to counsel. This society even though founded with strong religious foundations failed in many ways to teach the spiritual aspect of death. The innate survivor instinct of the human being finds it hard to accept the dying part of the earth process. Our surroundings dictate how we experience our first view of death whether it is our pets, people we know or loved ones. Society plays the role of setting ceremonies and rituals, which influence how we think of dying. Usually we find this through religious teachings. We form our spiritual beliefs about passing on from all of our experiences, but at times we may become confused. Religions in their preaching and teaching alter the interpretations at many points. We must evaluate what is relevant to our own beliefs.

When Mama Garner accepted dying as a part of life and living I trusted the physical body had ceased and the soul moved into another dimension. She was forming my belief system through her illustration. It was a comforting feeling. We are human so we grieve the loss of the physical presence of our loved ones. We want to see them walk through the door and hear them call our name and reach for their hand. Knowing their spirit is still with us can't erase the longing for them. We feel empty especially if a parent loses a child.

What experiences have formed your belief about death?

Premonitions

A Sense Of Knowing

Nancy had a bright smile but she had cried many tears as a mother. Her older daughter suffered with a disease, which she feared will probably end her life in her thirties. Her next daughter had developmental problems and Nancy struggled throughout the childhood and into the adult life with her.

Then came James, a bouncing, healthy baby boy.

There was definitely a soul connection between James and Nancy, obvious from the beginning. They talked and laughed and played, and he was growing. He seemed older than his years in many ways, walking early and talking early. James was a fast-paced child, never still, always smiling, and curious.

Nancy turned cold one day as she watched two-year-old James playing on the floor. She had a premonition James would not grow up. She had the feeling she would lose him early. Nancy pushed it out of her mind; it was an impossible thought.

James loved learning so school was a breeze for him. He was the spark in the family, forever creating some excitement and chaos all at the same time. The astonishing bond between mother and son only grew stronger. There was a special energy around James when the premonition she had sensed when he was two years old came again to her. Fear griped her. Was this a message or a warning? She couldn't tell and she couldn't accept it either. James was too full of life.

James was always a kid with a sense of knowing. In a passing conversation James said he didn't think he would grow to be an old man. Nancy's heart sank. Where would he get such an idea? The frightening feeling of Nancy's premonition came flooding back. She felt heartsick to even consider life without James. She pushed the thought out of her head once again and reassured him he would be an old man on the front porch in a rocking chair.

James was a live wire growing up, into everything, rousing everyone around him. James touched every life. If you knew James you remembered the special energy he shared. He was as typical as any teen finding his way through life, exploring every inch of the world around him.

Nancy and James knew they had been in other lives together. Both were recognizing their sixth sense was increasing. They were listening to their angels more and more. Nancy called it her voices, and she listened to them with her heart.

In March 1998 as they shopped the mall a book caught their eye in the store window. Nancy knew without a doubt she had to have the book. She picked up the book to find out why she was "told" to read it and was surprised by the title. Her Catholic upbringing made her stop. The title was *Talking To Heaven* by James Van Praagh. Would this book challenge her belief system? She didn't question the voices. Nancy knew the book had a message for her. She shared with James what she was learning in the book. It was forcing her to reexamine her beliefs and opening her to new ones. She told James about spirits of those who had passed giving messages to those left here. It was teaching her when people die they leave the body, but the spirit lives on. There is still the connection of love.

James said, “Mom, if you died you’d stay with me and if I died you would sure know I was around!”

James was leading a busy teenage life, thinking about graduation and how he would take on the whole world. Nancy had cautioned James about being around a certain group of kids. She had an uneasy feeling and couldn’t put her finger on it. James agreed he wouldn’t hang out with them. As teens often do, they make poor choices. In the heat of the moment, influenced by their peers, they don’t think. Teens living in the shadow of adulthood may act first, thinking only afterward of consequences. The gang had gathered; James happened by the apartment. The premonition was playing out. One month from the time Nancy had brought the book, James was dead.

It was after midnight when the doorbell rang. They awoke, confused. Was it the doorbell at this hour? Where was James? Nancy’s blood ran cold. She joined her husband as she heard a strange man’s voice coming from the front door. Her heart felt as thought it had stopped. In the doorway stood a policeman. Her ears heard the words, but comprehending it was unbearable. She kept thinking it had to be a dream. He was saying James was in the emergency room.

He had gone by the apartment after school where several boys were turning up the stereo and hanging out, typical of teens “cutting up and horsing around.” As James turned to leave one of the teens said, “Freeze, give me your money." He pointed the gun at him and pulled the trigger. It fired and James fell. A joke had gone terribly wrong. This accident would be a profound tragedy affecting many. Everyone's lives would be forever changed by James' death.

The premonition was real and no one would understand why. It couldn't be changed or prevented; the angels surrounded them in their grief.

The bullet hit him in the back of his rib cage, but didn't exit, which meant it completely exploded within his chest. The wound wasn't typical; it should have gone straight through which would have given him a chance to live. The bullet didn't exit. James had seen this day long ago in his premonition. Nancy could only ask why?

Everyone was devastated. James was gone before he had even lived. Why couldn't they have prevented this? How would they ever get past this? How do you heal from losing a child? The pain was overwhelming.

They left the hospital in a daze. How could their lives be turned completely into darkness in seconds? She didn't remember driving from the hospital. Nancy reached home and walked into his room. At once she felt James touching her. He was with her. She heard him clearly say to her, "Mom, I am so sorry." The words from the book were coming back to her. She was looking for signs. James was talking to her from heaven.

Nancy talked aloud to James and asked for signals just as they had read in the book. As she prepared to run her bath she instantly smelled the favorite cologne James wore. She smiled through tear-filled eyes. She knew he was showing her he was there.

Beth, her sister, said, "We know James is around

us." Beth told Nancy, during the sleepless night, she lay in her bed thinking of James. Christopher, Nancy's thirteen-year-old grandson was asleep in his sleeping bag on the floor beside her bed. All at once Christopher bolted upright and yelled, "Cut it out, James!" He told her James was doing the annoying thing he always did to him…flicking his ear! Christopher told everyone later, when he went to view James at the funeral home, he flicked James on the ear and asked him how he liked it. The kids were still playing from this side to the other. This was another assurance of life continuing past death.

They prepared to bury their only son. Nancy went to his bedroom to pick out clothes with tears streaming down her face asking aloud, "Why, God?"

Some come to make an impact in life
and an even stronger impact with their death.

Nancy struggled to go on with her life. She missed James every minute. She went through all of the emotions possible. If she had only been stricter with his whereabouts, if she had only made other plans that day, if only the gun had been empty, if only they could have saved him…the grief was endless. She agreed with the saying you aren't supposed to bury your child. They should be here long after parents. She questioned everything.

Why had James come to earth knowing his stay was short? She remembered the premonitions they had both had and the times they discussed it. Nancy prayed constantly and her guides and angels embraced her. Nancy listened closely hoping to hear James. There were many signs and signals from James. She recognized his communications.

She knew her son was with her whenever she thought of him or talked about him. Of course, he played with her, too. He would bring things to her attention in funny ways to remind her he was truly there. Feathers would appear in strange places. She would smile and say thanks aloud to him. It gave her some comfort and helped to easy the unrelenting pain. James stayed very close to her, not earthbound, but there to be with her.

Another visit gave Nancy confirmation James was still as social as ever. His best friend, Carl was grieving; they were as close as brothers and it was hard to go on. James decided he would go bowling with the gang. He never wanted to miss anything. The midnight bowling was dedicated to James with all his friends gathered to remember him. James could make those strikes, but his best buddy, Carl struggled every time. Carl rolled the ball and it headed toward the gutter as usual…and then a funny thing happened. The bowling ball seemed to flip away from the gutter and hit the pins. It happened over and over…the ball would head to the gutter and something pulled it back into the lane! Everyone began to watch. They couldn't believe it. Carl exclaimed, "He's in my ball, he's in my ball!" Everyone cheered! James was his usual self…creating a scene!

Even as time passed, James was with Nancy. At times he teased and played with her, and there were many times he seemed to be protecting her. She needed his energy around her so he stayed close. He seemed to know his way around very well on the other side. He wasn't confined. James wasn't concerned about how he left earth or the circumstances surrounding his death. He was busy stirring things up on the other side.

Some wonderful things began to happen. Nancy came to the ShowCase gatherings often and James began coming through with messages. At first James gave Nancy answers. He helped her with problems she was handling. James wanted her to heal and gain some happiness. He was being a strong protector for his mom. He was there…teasing her, giving her advice, guiding her and loving her. He communicated through us with no effort. He was having a ball bringing people together. James was a strong catalyst between the dimensions.

Then some spectacular things began to happen during the ShowCase gatherings. James became the arranger between the worlds. It was his purpose now and he wasted no time. James brought through people from the other side whether he had known them before or not. James loved bringing them through so they could communicate with us. He would set them up and then hang out to watch what happened during the gathering. He watched the tearful, but happy visits and reunions. He was the ambassador to this world while being in the other. It was as though he were standing with us saying, "Look who I brought through this time!" And he wasn't finished surprising us.

Nancy recognized James had arranged it when she brought her friends to our session. Their mother didn't come. Whether the mother was skeptical or afraid or didn't want to deal with it wasn't clear, but the ten-year-old son and his nineteen-year-old sister came. Nancy knew connecting to the loved ones, in spirit, could ease the loss.

She brought the young boy and his sister in the hope they could make some connection to their father who had been struck and killed on a freeway one rainy night in

Seattle. His dad had been coming to his son in dreams. These were very vivid dreams, which meant his dad was eager to come through. James seemed to be standing close by as I began the session.

As I began, his name came through quickly. He was easily communicating as though he had been ready and waiting for this chance to let his kids know he was there and still loved them as much as ever. He showed me the red sweat pants everyone hated, but he clung to them wearing the ragged, tattered pair every day when he got home.

I asked, "Did he drink beer?"

As they laughed and said yes, he showed me a unique way he would hold the can (not a bottle) with the little finger underneath the bottom and his thumb over the top of the edge, which made it look like his hand was the handle on the can. We all laughed. His energy was dynamic and he was wound up. He instantly, as though he were "just showing off," turned a can of beer to show me he drank Miller Lite beer. Everyone laughed again. He showed me small strips of leather; he had made something from these strips of leather. He wasn't tying them. I couldn't see what it was. He was insistent I see what this object was. His son didn't say a word and pulled from his pocket a braided key chain of leather strips his dad had made. It had a small baseball attached to it. He and his dad were big baseball fans. And, his dad was his son's biggest fan attending all the little league games.

His sister hugged him, and they both smiled through their tears. It had to be real; no one had ever heard of holding a beer can the way he showed us. His dad had to be talking to us for so many explicit details to come through. Their dad was assuring them without a doubt he was there.

Maybe in another setting he would have given them some fatherly advice or told them to study for their math test or brush their teeth every night. Tonight he was just giving them hugs.

As I visualized him he looked to be the age he was at his passing. He was very talkative and enthusiastic in his communications to us. However, he was not wearing the red sweats with the holes and stains. Maybe his angels issued him new sweat pants in heaven. He was such a likeable soul we wanted him to stay and talk. He made us laugh through the tears.

When the session was over the group began to mingle. I gave the young son a hug and said, "Maybe you came tonight, so you would understand your dad talks to you while you are awake just like he did in your dreams."

"He will always be there to love you and help you whenever you need him," I added.

With a slight smile the young boy quietly answered, "I know. When the light is red I don't strike at the ball, when it is green I know I can hit it." His dad was showing him signals through red and green lights when to hit the baseball during his games. I felt a surge through my heart as the little boy smiled a really big smile. He knew his dad would never leave him. We all had tears. His blessing was our blessing.

Later I was told their mom came alone to another session with the group without revealing who she was and did get a reading. I prayed she got a message, which would help her heal.

I knew I would probably never see the son, his sister or the mom again and if one word coming through helped them move on, our purpose was done. I knew James was there as their guide. Nancy had led them to the group hoping they would grasp even a shred of healing for their hearts. The healing was uninterruptedly passed onto Nancy. The healing we all felt will never be forgotten.

But, the evening wasn't over. There was an insistent voice calling to me. The energy shifted. I scanned the room for this new energy pull.

"DAD… not daddy"

"DAD"… "DAD"… it was insistent. I was hearing the words repeated over and over.

I hadn't been able to begin the presentation in my usual way. As people gathered for the group session I would open by introducing those who would be giving messages during the ShowCase. I called it the ShowCase since I never knew what we would be experiencing during the evening. You have heard of "flying by the seat of your pants?" I flew by the wings of the angels around me.

I listened as they repeated, "Dad."

I could make no mistake of what I was hearing through my right ear. This man insisted he was only called Dad…not father…not daddy. I asked three ladies sitting almost one behind the other whose dad passed less than two years ago. He was average height, thin and a real character and was only called Dad. When I asked which Dad had died alone and away from home one lady's eyes filled with tears.

"Yes," Trudy whispered, "My dad, Gary, was in Reno." She didn't know exactly what happened, the desk clerks couldn't get a response. They called again and there was still no answer. They decided to enter his room. He was lying on the bed; he was gone. He appeared to have sat up and simply fell backwards. They couldn't figure out what had happened. They were not sure if he had died late March 5 or early on March 6, 1998.

Her dad had been there alone. As we listened to Trudy's dad talking incessantly, more images came through. He had hidden his money in his boots in his travels as a courier for a cruise line in Panama. He showed me bottles. These were definitely bottles of liquor…different shapes and sizes and designs. They were on a shelf, but the liquor had been drunk…this was a collection, not on a store shelf. Trudy confirmed he brought booze from all over the world during his travels and he, for sure, drank it. The bottles were very unique in many instances making a nice collection. He showed me a fat roll of money. It appeared he had won in the casino. The winnings were not found, but many people were in and out of the room when they discovered him.

Why was he coming through? Why was he being so insistent? He had something he wanted them to know. It was important they knew it was not what he had thought it would be. Dying wasn't death.

Ironically, Trudy had never had a reading or been to anything that concerned psychics or mediums. She had come with a friend. The date was July 1999, less than two years after his death. She had felt he had been with her. Once, as she was getting into her car, a crow sitting on the facade above her flicked rainwater from the edge, sprinkling her. She looked up and smiled. He had been there. Trudy knew he had put her car radio dial on a car-talk station. She turned the radio on and the program blared. She never listens to the station and certainly did not have a button set to it. It was her dad's favorite show.

He gave many messages during the session, messages Trudy knew she was to take to her mother. Her mother hadn't been ready to face any of the pain. She passed the messages on to her mother, but her mother wasn't ready. The blessing was that her mother after months passed began to process what had happened.

Time passed and Trudy contacted me. She said over time her mother accepted the messages he was trying to get through to her. She began to release the hurt so the healing could start. She had to get past the anger. She had to let go. Her mother began slowly to create a life again. This helped Trudy to heal, too. They were recognizing their angels for the first time.

The Story Goes On

I wrote the account of "Dad" because it was a story of healing. I didn't remember their names. I just recounted the messages. "Dad" wanted to get through to them. "Dad" orchestrated another connection.

As this book went into proofreading my friend Marsha said she would edit the first draft. I was very grateful. When she returned the manuscript, she had a question. "Do you know who the lady is who had "Dad" come through?" Marsha asked.

"No," I answered excitedly waiting for the name and details. She said she knew the lady and was there the night the messages came through. "Dad" was at it again.

Trudy called me, and of course, "Dad" was there. She caught me up on more details I had never known about. She had written down what I had "seen." Yes, as it came through in the reading, he would have needed bypass heart surgery. The autopsy showed he had died of a hemorrhage at the brain stem. She said he was as much of a character on the other side as he was on earth. She confided, her mom had met someone and was making a new life.

Then I heard her voice change. She started to tell me about Christmas time. It was December 23, 2001. She had escaped to the country – beautiful Mount Rainier. She was ready for the holiday and relaxing in the serene setting. She loved the night skies. The stars were like crystals in the pristine sky. It took her breath.

She had always watched the skies in wonderment. Her dad had worked at the Palomar Observatory, so astronomy was a natural curiosity. Trudy was glad to be on the mountain. She pulled her coat tight around her in the cold night air. This was a special place and heaven seemed very close.

"Well, Dad, if you ever wanted to give me a sign this is the place." She paused and then gasped in astonishment — a beautiful shooting star streaked against the midnight sky falling behind the snow-covered mountain.

"Merry Christmas, Dad."

You only have to ask...angels listen, too.

"You know one of the messages the first night was 'it wasn't what I expected'?" Trudy said.

I barely remember what I said. I can reconnect to the readings, but it is not thorough memory. I must move into another level.

Trudy quietly asked if I knew what it meant now. Her dad was an atheist. He never expected a life after life. He didn't expect any love of God to be there, only nothingness. He had the surprise of his life, this one and the next, when the angels came for him.

After every session I left knowing why we were there. Everyone received energy and messages and inspiration during the evenings, but there was always one particular episode that stood out. We were blessed to share their time. The most precious gift was seeing the miracles, which came from hearing one sentence or maybe a simple phrase from a loved one.

One reassuring moment shared one more time helps heal the heart of those left behind. Some of the people I would never see again, but words they heard many times changed their lives forever. They would never be the same. Each connection to our angels and guides has a miracle connected for us.

When have your angels whispered to you?

Messages of Things to Come

At times we have to peel away the layers to see the reason. Some messages don't become clear right away, some take time to materialize. People ask questions. They want to hear what the angels have to say. Richard came often.

Richard was an energetic young man on the threshold of his life. He was a very loving, spiritual being with good intent as he brought various friends who had never been exposed to the intuitive arts to the ShowCase. His keen sense of humor endeared him to us all. He loved to watch their awestruck faces when they heard messages and details during their readings, things we shouldn't have known. Richard loved it. He knew they needed to hear the messages.

The ironic thing was Richard kept hearing one message over and over.

"Are you planning to go to New York?"

"No."

"Well, the energy of New York is very strong around you," I said.

No matter what other information came through it always included the question of New York. It was almost as though New York were calling Richard.

For months Richard came, brought new friends and listened. One night he admitted he kept thinking his grandmother might come through to him. He discovered when you talk aloud your angels listen to you! His angels brought her through.

His grandmother, Louise, was a real character. To say she was a little eccentric was a little understated. I described her appearance as she showed me how they played. She had wild hair styles and wore clothes, which were her own style. When he was very small she would balance him on her feet at his stomach, as she lay on her back, hoisting him in the air. Then he could play airplane and fly. They went for ice cream and entertained the parlor with the 'spoon hanging from you nose' trick. "Look, no hands," she laughed. It was obvious why Richard loved her so. He was delighted she had visited. And, she came again and again.

For months the pull to New York showed stronger and stronger until one night at the end of his reading I said to him, "It is as though the choice to go to New York is over, you have to go."

Richard smiled his cute grin and admitted, "I have my ticket to go this weekend. I fly Sunday." Richard arranged his work transfer to the Starbucks shop in lower Manhattan. He had his job, but no place to live.

Richard arrived in New York City on Sunday, September 9, 2001.

Then 9-11-2001 happened.

We were terrified for our country and worried about Richard. We learned Richard had transferred to the Starbucks, just blocks from the Twin Tower attacks so we were extremely worried. We realized he had to be in the center of the disaster. Finally, on Thursday, Richard left a message with his New York phone number. We were so relieved he was alive. We wanted to find out what happened and how he survived. His story was extraordinary.

"Richard, we are so glad to hear you are alive," I said when he answered. Yes, he confirmed he was about ten blocks from the attacks directly across from St. Vincent's Hospital where the injured and dead were being taken. His store virtually closed for business and began helping the victims. He had truly gone through a life changing experience as he watched destruction and death overwhelm the world as he knew it. His voice revealed the grieving.

Before hanging up he gently laughed and asked, "I survived, but will I find a place to live?"

"Yes, but, please, tell everyone you are helping and coming in contact with you need a place," I replied. The days following were filled with feeding the rescue workers, firemen and policemen and keeping water supplied to them. Everyone gathered incredible strength and pulled together to survive the disaster, which touched us all. The living had to go on.

I saw Richard would be taken care of. He only had to let people know what he needed as he was in the midst of helping others. He was doing what God had led him to do…helping others, so he would be taken care of as well. He was very strong in knowing it was meant for him to be in New York City, in lower Manhattan, in the shadow of the towers during those devastating acts of horror.

The next message, I got from Richard, confirmed all he believed. He had, indeed, found a home and was making new friends amid the chaos and sorrow. There were new job opportunities coming and ideas of future career possibilities. Richard's angels were probably working overtime, and he was listening closely.

God orchestrates our lives to put us on a path offering opportunities to evolve.

October 25, 2001 I received this inspiring email from Richard.

> "I have to say, it's very comforting knowing you're there…all of you. I'm still in a state of bliss. I LOVE it here. Funny though, I finally, after a year and three months, had come to a place in my life where I was perfectly content with being single…and you have to go and email me about meeting someone. (In your last email, not this one.) Anyway, I've told myself to stay open, clear and let whatever happens, happen. I know I'm in the right place and am ready for whatever life has to offer me. I am talking to a casting director next week about possibly going into some type of commercial work. What do you think? Also, I'm talking to someone about possibly going into public relations work.
>
> Exploring is fun…facing fears is fun!
>
> I hope you are using me as an example of what can happen, and what joy can come to your life when you take that LEAP!!!
>
> Never Better
> Richard"

To think someone caught in the midst of death, dying, and destruction found life and hope and faith is only one of the miracles that was born that day.

This story had begun at our meetings and it touches us still. There are email messages to stay in touch, and I always smile. Richard's leap was one of faith; his angels had prepared a soft landing though a maze of terror.

The Time Had Come

Sherrel's cousin read about the expo held at a mall in Tacoma, Washington. It would be their day out, and they were curious. It would be a fun weekend of exhibits and lectures and workshops. They found the ShowCase as though it were meant to be. They had no idea the ShowCase workshop would open a whole new world of awareness. Sherrel's life would never be the same.

Sherrel listened to everyone's reading around her in complete astonishment. This was a first for her. She found the readings curious and was amazed at how they unfolded. Watching the crowd's reactions she knew those who were "getting" it. She thought the things they heard confused some. When a session ends people will invariably begin remembering what they couldn't remember during the reading. We call this psychic amnesia…in the moment they can't remember their grandmother's name. For instance the name John means nothing until they remember it is their uncle. They can't remember information such as where they lived at age seven. People linger and give me feedback as they begin to remember more and more of what they heard during the session. They start to make surprising connections. As it becomes clear to them they are truly elated. Sherrel was among those remaining to ask questions and give some follow up. She was learning the links, which connect the past lives to this lifetime.

Our meeting was reuniting us to discover many shared past lives as Indians, pioneers, and as island dwellers. This was another synchronicity of the universe bringing us together. The purpose to reconnect and remember the experiences, choices, lessons, and growth.

Past life remembrance is life-changing.

Messages come when we are ready to hear and pull up past lives, as we are ready to deal with them. At each turn our angels gently guide us.

"I want a reading with you," Sherrel said as the crowd slowly filtered into the hallway from the seminar. Sherrel was small with a friendly and loving face, and there was a clandestine sadness in her eyes. I could see the weight of the pain she carried. She had held the pain so long, the familiar ache felt like a part of her.

I rarely did private appointments at seminars and expos, and I had no plans to do readings as I left the room. However, there was a special energy about Sherrel. There was this unexplainable sense of having known her before, a strange connection between us. I asked she give me a half hour before meeting me back at my booth. I have always known things happen as they are meant to be. There are no accidents. There was no question I would have a message Sherrel needed to hear.

A little nervous, she sat across from me and smiled as she said, "I don't know what I'm doing." I laughingly confessed I didn't know what I was doing either, but Spirit knew. Even though Sherrel had never had a reading she was spiritually open, not merely curious, but excited to hear what might come through.

She waited as I began to clear the energy around us. I began by listening to my breathing. I started to shift my consciousness, feeling the absence of the physical body, while attuning to hear their whispers. It feels as though I have floated into a mist asking anyone who has information to relay it to me. I ask for messages, which needed to be heard. As I prepare it sounds like rushes as wings, the indescribable sound of feathers in motion. I know the angels are here.

> In a silent prayer, "I ask for protection of white light to surround us bringing through only that of light and love." They "showed" me a scene. I knew I was seeing Sherrel.
>
> "You don't like to wear anything on your head," I began. Sherrel laughed in total agreement. I could see her in the past life as a despondent pioneer wife, alone and in a desperate situation. She was left in a desolate, barren land defenseless against the threat of Indians, the elements, and dwindling food supplies. They had made it this far, but their dream of a new land was lost. Her husband rode his horse over the wind-swept hills to hunt for food. He wasn't coming back for her. He died on the hunting expedition. She would never know what happened to him. The bonnet and dress she wore were a traditional printed calico, long since new, now faded and tattered, the last of her possessions.Her life faded as well on that bleak wind-swept prairie.

Sherrel now knew why she had an aversion to floral printed dresses and bonnets. In this life, covering her head with a cap, scarf or hat, especially if it were a print, had no place in her wardrobe. She wanted to leave the image and the sorrow of that lifetime behind.

He had left to hunt for a deer and game, but he never came back to her. The love she lost in that lifetime would come back to her in many lives.

I asked her to shuffle the deck of cards to continue the reading. The cards are used as a tool to gain more information. It is easier for many to accept a message if it is "in the cards" rather than from "out of the blue" using the sixth sense. We tend to be logical beings who need to see and touch proof of what we are being told. Shuffling the cards focused her energy, as she concentrated on what she wanted to know. As she handled the cards a single card literally flew out of the deck onto the table. As she reached to put it back in the deck I held her hand for a split second to see what the card was. It was the ten of hearts, a further sign she had been brought true love in this life.

Sherrel returned it in the deck, finishing the shuffle, and then placed them in three stacks. As the first three cards were turned over for the reading the ten of hearts immediately fell directly in the middle. Listening for information I tune in to all signs, which will bring a message. The ten of hearts represented a love with true heart connections. Sherrel acknowledged her marriage was a true love story. The moment they saw each other the recognition was unquestionable. It was a sense they had known each other forever. The cards Sherrel had chosen simply reaffirmed they were soulmates and meant to reunite in this lifetime.

Sherrel had been through some early relationships in which she had barely survived emotionally as well as physically. She was young and she fought with all her strength to get away from them. She succeeded in changing her life through sheer determination.

When Sherrel met Ron everything changed. It was

instant and the attraction was mutually strong. It was a remembrance of their other lives together with similar patterns in work, timing and actual situations repeating themselves. When they met Ron was a tugboat captain. Many of Ron's past lives were spent on trade ships, cargo barges, and fishing boats. It was appropriate they married on a boat at a rock quarry. As in the "what went before" times they lived to repeat many of the same events.

This time his boat was a high tech tugboat operation, towing in the fishing boats, cargo ships, and barges. This time he came home more often to his wife and three babies. They had time to spend as a family. In the other life he and his crewmates were gone for long periods of time on their sailing ships. Sherrel's days and nights were spent waiting for the glimpse of their sails on the far horizon. Although this life mimicked the others, it was far happier. There was more time together than waiting.

With her first pregnancy Sherrel's cousin recommended Kev Byden, a great family physician, for her care and delivery. She made an appointment and showed up for her first visit. Sherrel was astonished by the feeling she had when Dr. Byden held out his hand to introduce himself. She felt a strong emotion as though she had known him before. It confused her. Two more pregnancies assured almost six years of being in Dr. Byden's care. A friendship developed and Sherrel learned more and more about him. He loved the water and even more he loved to be under the water. Every minute away from his practice was spent in his scuba gear combing the depths of area waters. In his travels Kev found beautiful waters to explore, the waters of Hawaii being a favorite.

Kev Byden's underwater filming was a gift to anyone who watched the serene panorama of fish, sea life, and dancing vegetation as he glided through the waters of the sound. It was as though he left this world and escaped into another realm. He became part of the environment. He felt with little effort he could swim and breathe as the dolphins or the whales did often leaving his mask behind. He felt he was in the most spiritual place on earth. He felt the peace of the surroundings was indescribable, lacking words. On top of the water he filmed the orcas as they plunged into the depths and leapt into the air with their sounds echoing across the sparkling blue waters. He healed people in his practice, but his healing was staying under the water in the other world, his world.

Sherrel felt safe in the care of Dr. Byden and even her husband, Ron, bonded with him in a special way. With a lot of time away from home on the tugboats Ron was glad Sherrel had a caring doctor. There was a special attention Dr. Byden paid to them, and a closeness formed with them. Sherrel had a hard time defining the feeling she had for Dr. Kev Byden. It couldn't be misunderstood because she loved Ron intensely and was completely happy in her life, but there was a disquieting emotion she couldn't figure out. She couldn't put her finger on the connection, but it was unmistakably there. The second baby girl came and Dr. Byden shared in their happiness.

Sherrel and Ron watched their two girls growing and were looking forward to their third baby due in September 1997. Extra assignments kept Ron gone for extended periods, making it difficult for them during this pregnancy. Sherrel struggled near the end of the pregnancy and Dr. Byden kept a close eye on her progress. Ron was worried, but confident with her being in Dr. Byden's care. During her checkups Dr. Byden would sit in the floor and play with Camy and Susan. He had a special affection for the girls, again, making the close bond apparent. Sherrel couldn't understand why he would hold them and rock them as though they were his. She felt the love he had for the girls and it confused her even more, how close they all felt together.

Alisa Diane was born in early September. The birth wasn't easy. Sherrel had suffered internal tears because of the baby's position. The urgency of stopping the bleeding was the first concern. The other emergency was the baby's difficulty in breathing and a stomach disorder. Dr. Byden worked frantically. He held the new baby and tears filled his eyes. Watching you might have thought it was his newborn. Dr. Byden and Ron talked during the delivery about the difficulty and what procedures would be necessary. It was hours before the seriousness passed. Finally, Dr. Byden was confident the two were out of danger. The night passed and Sherrel and her new baby were improving rapidly. Everyone relaxed.

At one point Sherrel lay resting after the delivery. Dr. Byden was pointing out to Ron the superb stitches he had performed on her. I'm certain Dr. Byden's expertise came from his past life of stitching sails on their sailing ships. It was a remembered ability gained from sewing sails during the other lives where he and Ron sailed together. And, they probably admired each other's work in that lifetime, too. Sherrel remembers their inspection of her stitches and laughs. It was as though she weren't there as they discussed her condition. They seemed like partners on a mission even then. She felt like a project. She definitely felt cared for and loved.

It was time for her first visit to Dr. Byden for her and the baby after the delivery. Alisa was improving and seemed to be sleeping and eating, as she should. During Sherrel's full check up Dr. Byden found a spot on her lung x-ray, which frightened him. He called her right away to do further tests. Dr. Byden was insistent Sherrel take extra precautions. He took it much more seriously than she. He insisted she not go back to smoking after her delivery, but she slipped back into the habit. He kept checking Sherrel's lungs until he was confident she was not developing a health problem. All the while Dr. Byden was strongly urging her to stop smoking. He never let up on the warnings. Dr. Byden made Sherrel promise to give up the cigarettes. She promised. She began to regain her strength.

Alisa made slow progress in her young life. Her lungs were getting stronger and she was gaining weight. Sherrel's tests showed no malignancy. Dr. Byden was harsh in his warning to her. She would smile, say she would stop then she would weaken and continue smoking.

As time passed Sherrel grew stronger and Alisa, now eight months old, was rallying. At her check ups Dr. Byden was pleased with their progress. Sherrel and Alisa were past the high-risk stage and making improvement. Dr. Byden was happy with their progress and monitored their health.

Dr. Byden was revisiting his past lives and bringing closure. He had watched those he loved die from injuries, diseases and childbirth making him feel totally helpless then. He had the power to change it in this lifetime. As a physician, he had the power to heal. Dr. Byden had traveled his road well. He remembered the past, learned from it and came in to change it this time. He overcame the helplessness he had experienced in the other life by becoming the healer. Dr. Byden had completion.

His work was his purpose, but his passion was diving to comb the depths of the ocean. His hours away from the office were spent filming the marvels, which lay in the cold waters. There was a restlessness about him in those days. Those around him noticed it. They couldn't explain it, but they all felt the uneasiness.

Sherrel was alone when she received the call. It was from her cousin. She would never forget the phone call. She was stunned and in disbelief as she heard the words. The call came from same cousin who had recommended Dr. Byden to Sherrel. On a fateful day in June 1998 the call stunned Sherrel with the words, "Dr. Byden is dead."

Dr. Kev Byden was dead at forty-six. It seemed his life was in perfect order, there was so much ahead.

It was a devastating message. Sherrel was traumatized nearly collapsing. It was more than she could comprehend. She called Ron. She and Ron were in disbelief. They were grieving deeply. He couldn't be gone. He was far too young.

Kev Byden had donned his scuba gear and guided his boat across the waters just off the harbor. It was a wonderful day for diving with the eagles soaring near their nests in the nearby trees along the shore. Kev scanned the placid waters hoping he might glimpse an orca breaking the surface. He had filmed hours of their gliding gracefully in and out of the blue waters with their reverberations echoing across the placid surface. This was a place he could stay forever. This was home. He felt as though he were in the wrong dimension on top of the water. He felt part of the very elements that surrounded him. It felt strange to have to wear scuba gear. Kev had a bizarre thought, maybe he could actually breathe underwater.

Kev had taken his camera and slipped over the side of the boat into his world. He descended looking about him through the lenses of his camera as it began to capture the awe-inspiring universe below the surface. Watching his film tells it all.

His movement was effortless as he focused on one scene after another filled with serene beauty. An eel darts away. A lone fish poised ready to make lunch of a smaller fish was oblivious to his presence. One weird looking fish hides with only his large mouth protruding from a crevice in the rocks. Nearby are water plants swaying gracefully with the currents. Kev filmed almost as though he were caressing the sights of all that was around him. Kev was drinking in every spectacle as the light of his camera equipment swept the rocks and multitude of sea life swimming about him.

Minutes went by as the film rolled. In half an hour or more a large school of colorful fishes danced past and seemed to beacon him to follow. The shafts of light from above made it seem like a band of angels flying upward through the sparks of the water. It was a heavenly vision.

As the lenses swept both right and left Kev glided gently along seemingly not to disturb the world he was exploring. His camera focused on an anemone snuggled against a rock as though it were waiting for him. He approached with a reverence coming ever closer and closer catching the beautiful pink color of the sea creature. Kev lingered until his picture was a brilliant close up with the anemone filling the frame. The slight movement of the anemone looked like a beautiful pink rose caressed by a gentle breeze. It was an extraordinary scene only God could have created. There was a spiritual peace, which could only be captured on film — there were no words to describe it. Kev captured the tranquility he felt in this place.

There was a pause as though Kev had stopped his movement. It seemed out of the ordinary, not his usual method of filming. Briefly his arm appeared in the frame then the camera seemed to settle on the bottom. The film was rolling, but all movement ceased. There was no sight of Kev. There was no disturbance. Everything just stopped.

Above in the boat no one was aware anything was wrong. Time went by, too much time. Was it a regulator? Was he too deep? Did he have an attack of some kind? What happened? There were no answers.

Ron and Sherrel attended the service in the harbor honoring his passing. Their grief seemed unbearable. The depth of her grief perplexed Sherrel. As they stood casting flowers into the water near the spot where he had passed Sherrel felt a strange sensation Kev was there. The orcas appeared in the distance and their calls carried across the water. At the very moment an eagle appeared slowly circling over the spot where the flowers gently floated. Surely Kev was seeing all that was happening

The following days were difficult. The office staff was stunned. His parents were in shock. They had lost their only son. A beautiful human being who nurtured and healed so many, who loved the depths of the oceans and cared so deeply had left a big hole in the hearts of many people.

Sherrel cried many tears. The loss devastated her. She had lost her caretaker and their family doctor. The feeling of bereavement was overwhelming. Her three little girls lost their loving doctor. The two older girls missed him and didn't understand he wouldn't be there anymore. Sherrel gently explained he had gone to heaven. She helped pack his things at the office and went through his collection of pictures and tapes of his scenery beneath the waters. It only served to remind them of his love of the world below the surface of the sound, ironically he had taken his last breath in this spiritual place.

Months passed Sherrel couldn't shake the feelings. She mourned. Why was it so agonizing? There was a very real sense of heartfelt pain because of his death for Sherrel and Ron. They were close and this felt as though they were linked. The grief was continuous with few days free of the thoughts and reminders of Kev being gone. Ron was aware of the suffering Sherrel was going through. He tried to comfort her, but didn't know what to say since she was very confused about why she felt so sad. It felt strange her feelings were so intense. The months following his death didn't seem to get any easier for her. The heart of the strong emotion was a mystery.

Angels lead the way when the time has come.

It was time to reveal the heart connection. The angels had prepared the way. The reading progressed and the discoveries were revealing the links between them all. There were some astonishing connections opened up. It began to make sense. Sherrel began to recognize the feelings she couldn't explain were past life interactions. The information unfolded showing many lives centered around Ron and Kev being connected to the seas. Sherrel, Ron, their daughters and Kev had been together many times before.

There was always a link to the water. In one life Sherrel was the wife of Kev. Kev and Ron had a sailing ship. They seemed to sail the high seas as a trade ship going from coast to coast, bartering and dealing. If they weren't blood brothers they were as close as if they were. They worked side by side with precision. They were strong and had the ability to survive with their expertise and craftsmanship. They trusted each other whether it was in their trading expeditions or the defense of each other. Ron and Kev watched each other's backs. They had a solid partnership in an era that was ruthless and dangerous, where pirates wandered the high seas to take whatever you had. They had a powerful alliance in order to survive and provide for the family. The life of sailing kept them away for long periods of time. Sherrel was in a coastal village as the pregnant wife of Kev…they had two little girls with the third baby due at any time. She waited long, lonely days watching for their return. The wait was more distressing with the birth of their third due. She and her two babies waited. Kev and Ron were sailing home.

This part of the reading brought new explanations. Her face changed with each new revelation.

Kev and Ron arrived deep in the night. She was already in the care of the midwife in their small cabin near the shores. The contractions were intense. The labor was prolonged. In the lamplight it was apparent mother and baby were in serious trouble. The midwife (Viv, Sherrel's cousin in this life) could do little except hold her hand and massage her stomach as she bore down. Kev was in agony at his helplessness. Ron's concern was for them all. Kev watched in anguish, as her life was surely slipping away, leaving a baby girl without a mother. As Kev feared Sherrel died in childbirth leaving him to raise the three babies. It was natural for Ron to become a close second father to the girls. Ron had loved them all. These three baby girls seemed to be the ties in many lifetimes for Ron, Kev, and Sherrel.

Into another life, again, the ocean was the center of their existence. Ron and Kev owned the boat, which was built with their own hands. They were craftsmen in building their vessels. They were experts in sewing sails, mending them and keeping them in perfect condition. They were navigators to their very core. Knowing how to read the all the signs of nature such as the wind directions, currents, cloud patterns, and sky colors. Their voyages were the key to their livelihood. Sherrel, again, spent a lifetime waiting and watching for the boat to come in. She was lonely and she worried. There was constant danger.

The storm came out of nowhere. They had sailed into a surprise weather condition. It was a ferocious storm. The lightning and winds were unrelenting.was beaten and battered. They fought side by side to stay afloat. The struggle was a struggle for their lives. The boat was beaten and battered. The night was dark. The winds were tossing the boat violently when Kev was plunged into the cold waters through the fierce motion of the small fishing boat. As Ron held on for his life, he was paralyzed in his effort to save Kev who had disappeared underneath a violent, churning sea. Though injured and ill, Ron survived, limping home in the damaged boat to relay the devastating story of what had happened that fateful night. Ron felt guilty and helpless. Kev was a part of Ron. Ron grieved the loss of Kev. He was concerned about the family Kev was leaving behind, Sherrel and three little girls. On arriving in the village Ron had to find a way to tell Sherrel her husband Kev had died in the massive storm. He struggled with the words trying to assure her and the babies he would take care of them. He had loved Kev and he loved them. Over time, Ron proved his promise to Sherrel and the girls by providing a home and a safe haven for them. He struggled, but was able to keep them well fed and together. They eventually fell in love and married bringing a loving situation out of a painful happening.

This connection showed up again in the present lifetime. After Kev had passed Ron lost a tugboat project making it hard to provide as he always had. It was months before he was back on track and comfortable again. Again, the struggle was to take care of Sherrel and the three babies…and there was the loss of the boat in this life in a different manner, but nonetheless, it was a boat lost as before.

The soul connection between these people, Ron, Sherrel, Kev and the three little girls kept repeating lifetime after lifetime. The strands of all the lifetimes together were being interwoven once more in this time and space.

There was a time when I thought there was no reason to look into past lives. I was certain managing this life was enough challenge. After some explorations and new awareness I came to realize we are living the same lessons, the same tests and the same circumstances with many of the same people. Many people believe we live parallel lives.

Living again brings a gain in knowledge.

It was very obvious in Sherrel's sessions they were soulmates repeating the same events, at times in reverse roles, but it was the same pattern. She was beginning to glimpse how expansive our existence are. The reading was giving her an understanding she had never had. She had only felt the grief. The depth was seated in lifetime after lifetime of grieving. Awareness of this was allowing her to lift centuries of burdens. With the new understanding, she looked at dying in a different way. There is no death, but simply births into new lifetimes.

Sherrel had cried during the reading as she began to understand she shouldn't feel guilty about her feelings, which were strong and confusing in this lifetime. She stood up and we hugged. Her tears continued. These were healing tears. She breathed deeply and walked away. I knew I would see her again because I felt a very strong bond between us. I didn't even try to tap into our past life connection. I knew this would come in time.

In a short time Sherrel returned showing me a ceramic figurine of three orcas she just bought in the mall. She was sure the orcas represented her three little girls, another sign to her they were all connected. She told me her oldest daughter, not quite five years old, had written to Dr.

Byden after his death. Here is exactly what she asked her mom to write to him:

> "Dear Dr. Byden, I'll miss you very much. I love you so much. I wanted to be a little nurse and work with you for a few days. Now, I can't and it was going to be just you and me and the other nurses. It was going to be a very special day and now I'm very sad. The orcas make me think of you a lot. I wanted to show you my room because it is all sea life. Now, you'll never get to see it. Now, I'll have to tell all of my little orcas and they won't understand.
>
> Love, Camy."

Camy was young, but behaved older than her four years, and always had a lot to say about everything. After telling her mom what to write in her letter, she continued to share her thoughts with her. Sherrel had written everything in Camy exact words

> "When someone dies who is special like your best friend, but he's your doctor it's hard to understand when you're a little kid like me. Frizzle (her calico cat) tried to nuzzle me, but it didn't help. I'm so sad. I don't think it helps if you hug me either. Now he's gone so I'm sending him this stuff. It's not a lot of stuff just some flowers and pictures and some writing you (mom) wrote down for me because it is too much for me to write. Because it

> is a very sad day, but don't put it in the mail because he is in heaven. I'm just doing this for his own good because he is very special. I liked him a lot to where I loved him. I'll like my next doctor, but not like I loved Dr. Byden

"Dr. Byden loved the girls and they loved him," Sherrel said through her tears as all the old pain came up again. Sherrel held the orcas and the tears rolled down her cheeks as she remembered his love of the underwater miracles he caught on film and the orcas he followed above. In one of the scenes filmed only minutes before he died a large school of beautiful little fish swam like angels flying ahead of him leading him toward heaven. It was a profound scene looking back at it.

She returned again with another revelation as the puzzle pieces kept falling into place. Everything was connecting for her. And the tears kept coming. An amazing transformation was taking place within Sherrel. The sadness was lifting and her face was becoming brighter — she was even looking younger. The miracle of healing was visible.

We talked during the following weeks, which helped Sherrel fill in some blanks. More and more clarity brought tremendous healing. As each connection made sense to her she became more curious, however, making her want to know more.

Sherrel emailed me late one night:

> "As you can see, I, too stay up late. I always have, although I think that now it's more just to have 'me' time.

I can't remember if I told you about the reading I had from a man at the meeting. He said I had a life in Portugal. He said Kev and I had 7 kids! And he wasn't referring to baby goats! (Ron calls or emails me now & always tells me to kiss his baby goats.). Anyway, the reader said in that life Kev liked to help with the cooking & that he loved me deeply. That was it.

After I have another reading with you, or whatever you suggest, I would really like to be regressed. I need that for me. It seems like no matter how much I believe in you & everything that has come up, there is that little voice saying 'Are you sure that you aren't just wanting to have some kind of connection with Kev so badly that you believe everything that is said?'

It's so obvious it's what you want to hear, because you wear your heart on your sleeve. Even with all the connections I've made & yes, even all the goose bumps I wonder if I'm just imagining it.

Is this a common stage people go through? The doubting or cautious stage or something? It's strange I even have those thoughts because everything I have learned recently is exactly what I've always felt in my heart. Including what has surfaced with Kev. Everything just makes sense now. I have been thoroughly excited about all of it, & what's to come. So, why all of a sudden the little subconscious voice? I don't know.

> I'm not even sure why I' m even sending this to you. It's not like you're my psychiatrist or something. I do have a couple of people I could discuss this with, but for some reason it's you that's at the receiving end. Sorry about that. I actually don't understand a lot of what's going on with me right now, but it all feels so deep. Since the first day I met you, I have felt something is there, I just don't know what it is. I feel as though I have known you for an eternity, and you are very dear to me and close to my heart. You don't really know me, but I can count my dearest friends on about two fingers and those I have had for over twenty years. I have a lot of friends, but just two that I would trust with my life. With everything I have gone through in this life, I have never lost faith or doubted love. I find that amazing, even to myself; considering everything. I guess I just want you to know I'm not just some shallow, lonely person with nothing better to do than to bug you & take up your time. The LAST thing I want to do is to bother you & be a pain in the neck. So if I am, please speak up. I am by no means looking for a "free" ride. (No pun intended although it's kind of cute!) I do thank you. Love, Sherrel

It was very healthy for Sherrel to be skeptical. She was not being influenced or led by the reading. She was staying in control and keeping her power while exploring the details. Staying skeptical means you will listen and sense whether it feels right. This is your intuitive sense guiding you. It is listening to your angels.

Sherrel had asked questions and was finding answers. She was not dismissing what she heard in readings since the same details were coming up in different readings. It had to be repeated to help her grasp it. Yes, she wanted to hear there was a connection and the proof was — the words in the reading caused her goose bumps. The hair on her arms would actually stand straight up. This was one way her angels and guides could verify the message was true.

When our angels and guides are passing messages to us, some people may feel very cold, some get power surges of heat, and others get goose bumps. It is an outward verification of our physical body they are there and what we are getting in the messages is true.

Many people bring pictures of those they care about in this lifetime to find out what the connection was in the other lifetimes. We want to know about the relationship and connections of our husbands, fathers, wives, mothers, siblings, or grandparents. We wouldn't care about general acquaintances. I reassured her these are common feelings of questioning. Your intuitive sense won't fail you. An apprehensive feeling in your gut is a warning from your angels. Never ignore the signals. Sherrel was learning a new valuable lesson. She was learning to trust her own psychic impressions.

Sherrel's strong desire to uncover more specifics led to booking a private session for a past life regression. She was excited.

Sherrel had never been hypnotized so her trusting me was vital. She had to be comfortable with me. This is a gentle process taking her first into a meditative state. I assured Sherrel she was in total control and would remember everything. She had to be willing to go into the past life without apprehension to allow her to revisit the correct lifetime. Many people believe we have an exact number of past lives. Some believe we rotate genders. Most people think we return with soulmates to repeat unfinished business. We may return together to be rewarded in a lifetime for learning our lessons and evolving. Sherrel was ready to find out of if it was reward time.

The session began:

Sherrel positioned herself with pillows and covers so she would be completely comfortable as we began the relaxation. I asked her to start to breathe slowly and deeply creating a rhythm. She was to concentrate on her breathing, consciously listening, sensing the oxygen flowing into her blood stream filling her body with energy and healing. After a few minutes I asked her to feel her body becoming light and relaxed.

I continued to speak instructions in a monotonous voice to lead her into a hypnotic state; she was completely aware of all that was going on and in total control of her process. I asked her to feel herself floating, becoming lighter and lighter. At this point she was leaving her body becoming totally unaware of the physical. She was floating into the outer spaces becoming unconscious of her surroundings and her physical being.

She started to tell me how she was feeling and what she was experiencing as she progressed into another dimension. She was seeing bursts of light and felt a flying sensation. She could hear me and could tell me what was happening, but she was entirely oblivious to her body. I repeated affirmations telling her she was in a protection of light and love, reinforcing her subconscious trust so she would feel safe in her exploration of this strange, new realm. Sherrel followed my guidance floating upward into a universal space. She described seeing a triangle form of lights. She was enthralled. She wanted to linger. Sherrel had discovered the state of being out of her body and being in the universal realm while being totally aware of both places simultaneously. No experience compares once you have been there.

Sherrel had never been hypnotized, but she felt safe as we continued. She was eagerly searching each stage for the mysteries of her connection to past and present between her Ron, Kev, and her three little girls.

There was an excitement in her voice as she relayed what she was experiencing. In this phase she was totally unaware of her physical body, having a sense of floating freely through a still darkness with illuminating bursts of brilliant light all about her. There was a feeling of peace and calmness like no other she had ever felt.

I could "see" her joyfully absorbing each sight of her journey. I began to guide her in a gentle maneuver though the atmosphere, asking her to float toward earth. Talking softly in a hypnotic manner, I asked her to float until she could see the top of the clouds. I asked her to slip through the clouds, seeing the tops of trees as she continued to spiral toward earth. I guided her to slowly scan until she was drawn to a particular area of earth. I coaxed her to move toward a past life she needed to review. With much reluctance she ascended through the clouds, past the treetops and sought out a place to return to the earth. It was several minutes before she began to speak aloud, to say she had touched the earth, her feet on the ground. There was a long pause as she surveyed her surroundings.

> "Look at your feet," I said asking her to explore what she saw.
>
> Slowly she began to describe what she was seeing, "I'm wearing handmade boots. They look rough."

I asked her what kind of dress it was.
She said, “It is a printed cotton dress probably made from flour sacks.”

Sherrel confessed she can’t stand print dresses in this lifetime. She continued searching the area. I told her to see herself walking up the path and follow it to where she lived. I asked her to tell me as soon as she saw the place. I could sense her moving toward the clearing in the meadow as the path sloped upward toward a cabin. I knew she would recognize it. It seemed to face the morning sun.

“Where are you now,” I inquired. She said she was approaching a cabin she knew was hers. I told her to climb the two steps and cross the porch to the front door. She agreed she was seeing the two steps and was opening the door. She saw the fireplace and the wooden eating table. The handmade furniture was in neat order. A quilt covered the wooden bed. She didn’t see windows and knew there was only the one door. The cabin was empty. Sherrel sensed she had no children. Her life felt very empty. There seemed to be no animals around the cabin. Chickens scratched in the dirt in back of the cabin clucking when the hawks and eagles swooped toward the ground.

“Is the rifle over the fireplace?” I asked.
Her answer was curt as though it were a dumb question, “No, it was hanging over the door.”
“Did you ever use it?” “Yes, once.”

She was waiting for him and she knew he'd never come back. Her husband Ron had crossed the meadow heading into the trees for a hunting trip to bring back food. She was alone, and she was lonely as she watched and waited. It had been months now. She walked from the cabin through the tall grasses following the path he had taken hoping she would glimpse something…anything. Suddenly she saw the pack of wolves crouching at the edge of the thickets. If she turned to run she would never reach the cabin before they attacked. She froze with fear watching at least nine or ten as they were beginning to stalk her. As she cautiously began to back away, she raised the Winchester she had brought from over the door. The only chance was to kill the pack leader. They began to move toward her. She squeezed the trigger and the shot sounded like an explosion in the quiet of the meadow. The lead wolf dropped. The pack scattered into the brush.

She was terrified as she ran as fast as she could go toward the cabin. Carrying the rifle caused her to stumble as her skirt caught her foot on the step of the porch. She tripped falling into the doorway bashing the right side of her head. She was still shaking as she feverishly tried to close the door. Her wound was severe and took months to heal. From that time on she rarely strayed very far from her cabin. I sensed she died alone in the cabin. She was seeing this lifetime as you would a dream, vivid and detailed. I saw her energy shift.

I physically watched as her face aged with sadness. This was an image you would have been able to see if you had been in the room. It appears like a photographic negative crossing her face letting you see what she is seeing. Many people who sit in on the regressions see these images. They move quickly across their face, like a slide show, giving glimpses of the physical bodies they had known in other times. I have watched — in color — male faces, female faces, young, old, fat, thin, and decorated faces reveal images of the past incarnations.

Many have witnessed seeing only pure white light where the physical body is positioned in their chair. It is as though the molecules of the body have dissipated leaving only the energy of the spirit. It is in spirit. Those sitting will feel a physical sensation. After the session is over and they are back "in their body" they will recall feeling a change in physical shift at this point of the session. It is an extraordinary sight for those watching and even more so for the person sitting. It is an unforgettable awareness never before felt by most. It is a place they can forever return to in an instant. It becomes a means of healing.

I watched the sad, aged face begin to fade. She had to observe the experience in order to move past it. I knew her life ended in loneliness without her love beside her. Sherrel had replayed the same scenario over and over.

Her energy began to shift. Sherrel was leaving this life review. I asked she take any healing she needed into her physical body as she rose above the setting of that life. She could leave the pain of that lifetime behind, as well as the loneliness and the waiting. I asked her to leave the lifetime knowing she didn't have to revisit it again.

I asked her to float, feeling very safe and comfortable as she scanned another vortex of energy. She was describing her feeling of floating above the earth as she searched for another place, which seemed familiar. She was silent for a few minutes before sensing another lifetime she needed to remember. I asked her to float down into that lifetime.

> "Where are you walking?" She wore a sarong of blues and greens walking barefoot along the beach lined with flower-laden foliage. It was paradise. She gathered shells and picked flowers below the mountain where the cliffs were bathed in sunshine and waterfalls flowed to the sea. She was no more than fourteen years old, but she was in love. She entwined grasses to braid ornaments to wear on her ankles. She watched the horizon and waited for his boat.
>
> Tanned by the tropical sun, he was muscular and strong from the diving he did to bring treasures from the ocean floor. He brought back fish he had speared to cook on the fires outside their huts.
>
> I asked Sherrel to walk the beach following the path to her hut. I asked her to look up the side of the mountain to the other huts nestled in the tropical paradise. She pointed to the one where her family lived. This was a loving family life. Her father, who helped her collect shells and a mother who taught her to make sarongs and jewelry from shells, loved her. She made leis of the fragrant blossoms. I asked her what the red flowers were she picked.
>
> "Hibiscus," she said at once.
>
> A parrot sat at the opening to the hut where her beloved laid. He was older and a powerful man in

the village. She lay with him on a mat, but wasn't allowed to stay. She was too young to be given to him in marriage. They were betrothed and she would wait many more months before they could be together. I asked if she recognized him. Who was he in this life?

"Kev," she said quietly.

Sherrel longed to stay in this lifetime, but her energy was being drawn away. Again, she was forced to wait for her love. She had revisited a beautiful lifetime with loving surroundings.

She felt blessed. She had reconnected with the family in this life. Kev, her betrothed in that lifetime, was her doctor in this lifetime. Her father and mother in that lifetime were father-in-law and mother-in-law in this present lifetime.

In This Lifetime

Lane and Grace had made a love story come true. After Lane's marriage to Ron's mother dissolved he met Grace. Their love grew and they agreed to marry. They found each other and found their paradise in Hawaii. Ron was happy for his dad. Grace was a stepmother, but she eventually felt like a mother to Ron and Sherrel. They visited when they could. It wasn't often enough since Ron and Sherrel lived on the mainland. Lane and Grace had many years together — happy years. They walked the beaches hand-in-hand. Lane collected shells. Grace fed the birds. Together they watched the horizons each night turn from red to golden to blue as the sun sank below the ocean's edge. It was their heaven on earth.

Then the heartbreaking news. Lane, Ron's father, passed. Grace was overwhelmed with Lane being gone. She was strong and independent, and capable of handling her life, but her heart was with Lane.

Ron and Sherrel did all they could. There were hours of calls back and forth from Hawaii. Grace and Sherrel discussed everything under heaven and earth and those things of the other side. They read books together. Grace was curious and interested in spiritual occurrences. Sherrel talked about what she had discovered in readings and past life regressions over the past year. They had talked about the communication to the other side, which John Edward did on his television gallery. Grace knew Lane was with her. To hear a message from him through human words would have gladdened her heart. She would have loved to have had a session with John Edward to hear a message from Lane. She missed Lane so much. Ron and Sherrel tried to fill the empty space in Grace's life with phone calls and letters to ease her sadness.

Grace talked to them all, chatted with the girls, and the love bond grew stronger. Grace mailed fun things to the girls and then they talked into the night about what was going on. Although the miles separated them, the feelings were close. Grace shared stories and the days past. Sherrel learned much from her. It was a warm feeling in Sherrel's heart to have Grace in her life.

Grace sent Sherrel a book of instructions in lei making. The book showed the braiding techniques of using grasses to create beautiful adornments to wear. One of the pictured braids looked exactly like the one Sherrel had worn on her ankle in the island life she had seen in the regression. Sherrel had made another connection — another puzzle piece. It was strange it had come through Grace.

Grace's health was failing. She told them she was doing well when they pried. She wouldn't say much. Losing Lane had taken its toll on her immune system and her spirit. She was, on an unconscious level, preparing to join Lane. Grace was putting things in order. She wanted them to come to Hawaii.

Sherrel and Ron arrived in Hawaii hoping to spend some quality time with Grace. They were stunned she was so weak. She had not revealed the truth of her condition. She was gravely ill. Lane had been gone for a year and it was just too lonely without him. They talked and visited. Sherrel read to her from Jonathan Livingston Seagull, one of Grace's favorites. Maybe it was reminding her she could fly. They reminisced, as Grace was growing weaker.

They sat with her. She was tired and she asked them to leave her alone. Ron and Sherrel felt helpless. They talked and walked the beach. They felt the energy of where Lane and Grace had walked leaving footprints in the sand, breathing in the ocean air while they strolled. It had been their heaven on earth, but heaven was where Lane was, and they felt Grace slipping away. Her eyes were closed most of the day as her breathing became shallow. This time was between her and God.

Sherrel picked the plumeria blossoms during each walk, putting them in the refrigerator for a collection; she wasn't sure why. She and Ron watched the sunsets. There was a heavy sadness, but at the same time she was going home.

Sherrel and Ron followed Grace's lead staying when she needed them, allowing her time when she wanted to be alone. With them there she seemed to relax. She seemed to have been waiting for them. Sherrel often sang a song close to her heart — the words made a promise of a time beyond time in a place of pure love. Sherrel knew she was meant to sing it for Grace. Before leaving the mainland she made a CD, not dreaming her angels were indeed orchestrating it.

Her friend Luke designed a rainbow label and made a CD recording of Sherrel singing *Way Over Yonder*. As Grace began to slip away Sherrel feared she wouldn't get to hear it. Sherrel gathered the flowers and began to string them — she knew how to make the lei from the book Grace had sent her. It was beautiful and the fragrance a heavenly scent.

By now Grace hadn't opened her eyes in many hours. She was unresponsive. Sherrel gently placed the lei around Grace and patted her lovingly. The song began to play. Grace was weak, and her eyes still closed as she heard the words begin. She gave a slight smile. Sherrel smiled through her tears as she saw Grace's toes move to the music. Grace was hearing the song. The angels were singing her to heaven. Sherrel had sung this song just for "Grace, from me to you with lots of love."

The first thing I'll see is the sun shining golden,
shining right down on me
Way over yonder
Is a place that I've seen
In a garden of wisdom from some long ago dream

A way over yonder…that's where I'm bound.

(Excerpted from Way Over Yonder by Carole King)

Aloha

Love Led The Way

Grace was bound to the land where Lane was waiting with open arms. Love led the way. The angels were singing.

Sherrel and Ron knew amid their tears Grace and Lane were together again and this was the silver lining. They would miss her as they had Lane. The girls would miss playing together in the waves with them. They wouldn't be there to walk the beaches when the moon was so bright it was like daylight. They would miss watching Grandma Grace feed her flock of colorful birds. They would all miss the long phone calls held late into the night.

Even through the sad tears Sherrel was watching for the spiritual messages. The messages came easily in the shells she found, in the fragrance of the blossoms, and the birds, which flew into the Lanai as though they knew Grace's spirit was still looking out for them. The various sizes and colors of birds flocked to her feeders. They flew above them along the beach. Grace was gone and the birds were still singing.

The birds and the angels knew Grace was still there.

Sherrel walked the beach wondering about it all. Was all of this a repeat of her other life on the island? Was this a déjà vu? The beach was familiar as she walked to where it curved into a cove. There was such a calm in her soul she knew the truth. The feeling of being loved was the same. The huts were condos this time. The flowers, the shells, the birds and the loving people were recognizable. Her mother and father were the same. She was here with her love, Ron. She caught her breath and noticed the chills made the hair on her arms stand straight up. Her angels were answering her questions. There was no doubt. And then, she knew Grace was there. Sherrel gazed across the blue waters and was surprised. Hawaii has few rainbows so as Sherrel stood in awe, seeing a complete rainbow lying low over the waters, she knew Grace was giving her a sure sign heaven was a wonderful place.

My phone rang and I knew it was Sherrel. She was flying back tomorrow while Ron stayed to take care of details. She said, "You know, this has been one of the worst years we have ever had. We had four deaths in less than two years. Ron changed jobs so our finances were tight until it was settled. Everything seemed to be a struggle. Then Grace was diagnosed with cancer and we were heartbroken. It seemed it would never end. But, you know, because of the spiritual awareness and the experiences I've had it has become one of the best years of my life."

Sherrel had taken the healing she had received and was passing it on to others. She told Grace what had happened to her, and how knowledge, awareness, and understanding had allowed her to move into totally new life energy, physically and emotionally. Her conversations were helping to heal others. She thought of Grace. Seeing the purpose of why things happen as they do, and accepting them, meant Sherrel was finding peace in her life. She felt the shift to another spiritual level. She was being an example to others especially her children. Their spirits were flourishing. She thought of Grace again.

The girls knew Grandma Grace was sick and knew she would go to heaven when she died. Coming back to tell them Grace had passed wasn't easy for her and Ron. The loving respect Ron and Sherrel had built throughout their marriage created a security few families have to face a crisis. Strength and compassion gave them the courage to talk honestly with the girls. Even though the girls were young, Ron and Sherrel knew if they told them openly the girls would grasp the part they needed to hear. It would help them understand the emotional time everyone was going through. As they started to speak, the girls began to softly cry. They reassured the girls Grace was still close to them in spirit and she was safe in heaven.

Their daughter Susan quietly said, "I went to see Grandma Grace last night."

"You did?" Sherrel asked excitedly. "Did you talk to her?"

"I just said 'I love you' to her," she smiled and her eyes filled with tears.

Susan had said a while back she flies at night and told Ron and Sherrel she could float around her room and see her body asleep on the bed. Time past and she told them she went downstairs. Again, they said this must be exciting. In turn, she had a question. "Do you think I could go through the walls?"

Her dad was reassuring as he said, "Sure you can, but take it slow the first time just in case it smarts a little." Susan felt confident as she skipped away to play. She hadn't mentioned it again until she told them she flew to see Grandma Grace. Alisa listened. Being the youngest she was struggling to understand what was going on.

Then she began to cry saying, “I can’t fly to see Grandma Grace ‘cause I don’t know how.” Her little face was so sad.

Susan gently took her hand and said, “That’s OK, Alisa. I’ll come and get you when I go, and I’ll hold your hand so you can fly, too.” Alisa paused through her tears and the girls hugged each other. They knew Grandma Grace would be waiting for them. It touched their hearts to see their little girls so loving and so accepting of living and dying, the faith of the innocent, as the Bible says...be as little children.

Sherrel had come to realize each experience is a learning experience. She had grasped something few people ever get. Their lives are forever changed. Sherrel and Ron with their three girls had found what their angels were holding for them. They heard the flutter of wings.

Keep Them Close to You

I wish I could tell you all of the stories...endless stories, which reveal the multi-dimensional ways our angels reach us, and how the messages correlate to every facet of our lives.

Each time I walk away from a session the purpose is obvious, the messages, and those they are to reach, are crystal clear. Many times the intent or the anticipated direction changes completely. I never question what takes place. They are there to hear what they need to hear which is not always what they want to hear. They may come asking about their job and a message concerning their health comes through. They might want to know about their love life, but their grandmother comes through to talk about a crisis in the family. It is obvious when we gather we create a vortex for the other side to communicate through. It is the opening for our guides and angels. It happens just as it did in the movie *Ghost.* All the spirits tried to come through the character of Whoopi who played the channel. They on the other side seek a venue to speak through. As we gather, the room fills with those wanting to contact us. Many entities gather in the room, some to give messages, while others observe.

In one instance, the farmer who had grown crops on the land beneath us came to visit. He was quiet and observing, wearing tan work clothes. He looked to be in his eighties. He was tall, straight, and strong even in those years. He seemed to be a proud man, proud of his work and his land. We sensed his openness to what we were doing, but he wasn't interested in participating. He just sat and listened. He seemed to have been alone in his last days and walked the fields in reverence for the earth. We never found anyone who knew who had owned the land. The only people who could remember when it was open, undeveloped country said several people had farmed the area. So, we just welcomed him to our gatherings and hoped he approved of our energy being there while hoping he would continue to visit.

One of the most memorable nights was when a grandmother named Alice kept whispering her name to me. These are the ones "who won't shut up." They will keep repeating until I recognize them. As I asked whom Alice was connected to, no one answered. I continued on — within minutes the whispered name of Alice came again.

"Alice wants to talk to someone," I repeated. Since it is difficult for people to recognize and recall names in the moment I waited, but no one remembered. The evening ended and we still didn't know who Alice was looking for.

We met the following evening and again she came through. This time Alice was recognized. Her granddaughter listened as I described her, her condition at passing, and some of her weird idiosyncrasies. "Oh, that's my grandmother," the granddaughter said smilingly.

"Well," I replied, "she came last night to talk you." We laughed and were then surprised as the granddaughter told us that she and her friends were, indeed, trying desperately to get there the previous night, but everything ran late and they missed being there. The grandmother knew they would be there. She wanted them to know she was with them. The love between them was a living memory.

I continually watch for signs and affirmations at every turn. I stay very conscious of all that is around me, and what the angels are telling me. Many times when I am working even the television music channels give me messages. The music is beautiful and only the name of the song with the artist's name is shown on the television screen. Some of my favorites are the CDs of angel music by Herb Ernst. The instrumental music helps as I prepare to write or to do readings. It creates a meditative state. At times I'm amazed when after hours of working I will be pulled to look at the title of the song playing — there is always a message in it for me. I smile, and whisper to my angels, "Thank you." They find an open channel and the means to speak to me. I choose to listen.

So, as I was writing the story about the farmer visiting on several occasions, I looked up. The music title was "Farmer's Hand" by Davidson from a CD of Celtic music. Do I think the farmer was with me? I know I was connecting to him or his angels. And it convinces me there is no time in their realm. He appeared at our meetings a few years back and when I was writing about him he was again available to me. I still don't know his name, but this is not important. Even though I don't know the name of this man, planting his fields, taking in his crops, and loving the land, he is not a stranger. Was he letting me know he still walked the land? Would he bring me a message? I would listen. Mama Garner had taught me this long ago. She was reminding me to make the connections.

Angels bring the message we need to hear...
repeating it until we hear them.

Mama Garner set my direction in life during those quiet evenings on their front porch. She had called them visions when she had foreseen things to come. To others she might say it was a dream since I never heard labels of being psychic or astral traveling or out-of-body experiences. I know this was what she was teaching me. Many of things I am, only now, coming to fully understand. Mama Garner taught me the difference between judgment and discernment.

Judgment is when I decide your behavior
is wrong and I expect you to change.

Discernment is when what you are doing is
wrong for me and I simply separate,
honoring your choice without participating.

I was to be an observer. She taught me to find the good in every seemingly disastrous event. It was difficult when the pain seemed endless and the situation unbearable. It was hard to see that it was happening for the best, but time always proved it to be true.

Another lesson was learning to listen
the first time the angels whispered.

Listen at the First Whisper

The lesson becomes more difficult each time the whispers are ignored.

Be reminded: you are going to do it until you get it — so listen the first time. Make the change while it is easy and you have choices. Prolonging the decision leaves you with no choice. Things will worsen until you are forced into a move. You soon come to realize you are creating each minute of your life by your choice and your state of mind.

In workshops I ask people to list all their complaints. This is usually an easy task. The things that aren't working are the first in our mind. They complete the list. Then they write what their part is in the situation. It instantly becomes clear how they set themselves up to live out the experience. By changing their behavior and perception they create a new path. If it isn't working, change it. Make a conscious choice.

The telling reality was when they were asked to go back to the initial point of their decision. It was back to the time they felt they should have made a better choice. This is the time when they knew it wasn't working. In other words, this was the time they had ignored all the messages their angels and guides were showing them. Then they realized they were living out the consequences of their decisions. At this point they could make a new decision, change the behavior, and create a whole new life.

I found another test:

If you knew you were going to die at sunset tomorrow what would you be doing?

I was surprised to watch as many had blank expressions. They had never thought of that scenario. Without knowing how they would spend their last day, they had no plan in place for their future. Without a focus our guides and angels can only wait. Ask and be specific; your guidance will be there. What we think and what we say has extreme power in what is manifested. So, be clear what you think and what you ask for. You will receive.

Ask for abundance in all things; ask for what is best for you and the universe.

Ask for joy in all you do. Create happiness. Happiness begins with laughter. Mama Garner and Daddy Babe taught me to laugh. Maybe it happened, but I can never remember their being angry. There were trying times, I'm sure. There were hardships to live through and heartaches. There were frustrating circumstances, but loud voices or cross words were not part of their life. They had a certain dignity in the way they handled stress and struggles. They dealt with the present, putting the past in proper prospective. They laughed together and stayed together.

Their way of life was probably responsible for the quality of their long life together. They had given me an awareness of what loving beings were — joyful, devoted, and at peace. I now realize the most child-like people, and those who are filled with laughter, are the most spiritual beings. These people have happy eyes, the windows to the soul. Maybe it is the trust they had in the higher power and the angels all around them. And maybe I needed them, so they stayed on earth a little longer.

In Daddy Babe's mid-eighties he began to deteriorate from the stroke he had suffered. His condition was becoming difficult and he was tiring of the physical. If his health worsened it was evident they would be separated. He was deciding he didn't want to stay. Things weren't going well, and his quality of life was degenerating.

Mama Garner felt what was happening. She understood and, in her own spiritual way, accepted it. She told me even though Daddy Babe's stroke had changed their lives drastically they had created a new life after it happened. Their time together was different, but it was a rewarding time full of talking, reminiscing, and laughing. He was no longer checking fences on the ranch, herding cattle or hauling a truckload of alfalfa hay. They were together and living every minute, enjoying their time together. They chose to look past the life problems. They perceived it as a happy time, and therefore, it was. Even those were good years for them.

Time was coming to an end. Daddy Babe was rushed to the hospital. Mama Garner whispered as we drove, "He won't come home this time." Maybe he knew, too. He looked at her with tears in his eyes as they wheeled him to the emergency room to determine if he had suffered a heart attack. Was he saying goodbye? We refused to think about it.

He was resting so everyone went home to try to sleep. We drove in silence, weary and saddened. We couldn't sleep. Mama Garner sat quietly. Everyone left the room. Finally in a whispered voice she said, "Babe isn't coming home. I had a vision of him walking into the hills of heaven."

I at once had the vision of a beautiful sunny day with Daddy Babe walking toward distance hills bathed in light and hazy blue clouds. It was a heavenly place. He was going home, back to pure love. I watched her release him to go, grieving, but accepting his will. We stayed by him for the next few days. It hurts so much when the love has been so very strong. Even a moment of this special gift is better than a lifetime without it. Many people live a lifetime never knowing this bond of love and harmony. We would miss him so. Daddy Babe passed never leaving the hospital just as she had seen in her vision.

Mama Garner remained independent moving to an apartment on the edge of town. I would visit and take her little gifts. She loved lacy linen handkerchiefs, and of course, flowers. She missed her flower filled yard with all types and colors. We took her to church nearby and had lunch afterwards. We took long drives on Sundays passing the ranches that had been home to us all. She would tell us how our family, from Wales and England, lived in North Carolina before settling in the middle of Texas. She told us lots of stories about our family's history of settling many of the frontiers. She was nearing the century mark so she had seen some amazing things in her lifetime. When she and her parents traveled through Dallas the streets were still dirt. Their travels in horse-drawn wagons and buggies crossed the hills into central Texas where their ranch was established. Mama Garner had many memories and fascinating stories to tell. We loved visiting to hear all the things she had seen in her years. It made us realize how much our world had changed in a short one hundred years. Her memory was sharp and with her sense of humor the stories were entertaining and educational.

Mama Garner stayed active and healthy. She took long walks and said people probably wondered, "What is that old lady doing out walking?" She helped the old ladies next door go for their mail down the road — they were in their mid seventies and she was in her early nineties — but they were the old ladies. She did out live them all.

One day as we sat visiting we were remembering the good times down by the lake — the time they were fishing and a big bass hit the line. Daddy Babe fell into the water's edge trying to land his fish. It was so muddy he got stuck. He couldn't get up. She tried to help him out and they began to laugh. The more they laughed the deeper they got into the mud. It took them quite a while to crawl back to the dry bank. They were both muddy from head to toe, and the fish got away, too. As we laughed I had an instant flashback of Daddy Babe and Mama Garner giggling. I could hear them. I looked at her twinkling eyes and blurted out, "You see him every night, don't you!"

She said with the same giggle, "Every night he is there."

On the astral level they were still together.
Love lives on, and the angels smile.

Mama Garner was teaching me again. There is no death. She and Daddy Babe would see each other on the other level and be together to laugh and love. The physical didn't matter. They were together in her dream state, on the astral level. We talked and she told me about visions she had. Maybe she didn't tell me all of what she saw, but she was again teaching me about death. Maybe she was preparing me without my realizing it.

My dad passed without warning.

He was only in his mid sixties, too young to die. He had always said he would go "with his boots on." He was riding in a cutting horse event when he felt ill. He left the arena and was rushed to the hospital. Within forty-five minutes he was gone apparently of a heart attack. We had driven furiously to get there calling for Care Flights and other doctors. Would we be better to move him to a cardiac center? It was a frantic and helpless feeling. We didn't know what to do. We were trying to make the right choices to save him. We were searching anxiously for help. But, we arrived too late. As we entered the emergency room he lay covered with a white sheet, but ironically, one boot was exposed. He died with his boots on and he was buried with those boots.

My mother was totally lost without him. They were with each other every day since they married. They both loved the ranch life and had taken every step together. She found life painful and couldn't bring herself to move his clothes or any of his belongings. She left everything in place. If she didn't move it she wouldn't have to face he was gone.

I tried to help fill the empty spots with daily calls and lots of visits. I made suggestions to travel and try some new hobbies. There was nothing to replace the life she had before. I tried to suggest ways to create another life, not to replace what she had, but to find some meaning. She at least went through the motions of trying to move forward.

As time passed her sadness seemed to overwhelm her. Mother was almost sleepwalking through her life now and it took a toll on her immune system. Her grief was constant and unrelenting. She was becoming weary. Her illness was diagnosed — it was cancer. Was she choosing to leave? My symbolic dream came shortly afterward.

Angels deliver messages through the dream state when our conscious mind has difficulty accepting or understanding what is to come.

In my dream I was in a huge crowd that was moving southeast toward a center, it felt like a park where people gathered. The day was gray, I saw no sun. I saw my dad flying a strange vehicle. It had no top, but looked and flew like a helicopter. My mother was quietly sitting beside him. There was no talking. I was standing with Mama Garner on the ground, feeling we would have to "go up" to get where we wanted to go. Mama Garner didn't want to leave the ground and was complaining. She didn't want to leave the ground! I kept talking to Mama Garner while watching them fly, thinking my dad would be able to keep the vehicle airborne. He was flying just above the crowd following them to the central place. Mama Garner and I talked, but there was no other communication. It was as if my mother and father were not aware of us at all. I turned to see Mama

Garner watching them. She wore a flower-printed blue and white dress. She stood just behind me and continued to refuse to get into the vehicle. She wasn't going and I knew I wasn't going.

I awoke very confused. This was a lucid dream meaning it was a distinct message. Lucid dreams are those dreams so detailed, so real, you can recall them years later, forgetting no part of it. Dreams come in symbols so I carefully considered what it was telling me. I knew my mother wanted to be with my dad, which was understandable. The vehicle symbolized their going to an upper level above the earth, with my dad guiding it. Mama Garner and I were outside the vehicle on the earth level. She was talking to me and observing the happenings. She and I knew we were to be left behind. The dream was telling me something.

Five days later we gathered for our 1987 annual family reunion and to celebrate Mama Garner's birthday. The weather was a perfect spring Sunday and the park was full of greenery and blossoms. I wanted to tell Mama Garner about my dream and see what she felt it was telling me. I was amazed as she got out of the car. Mama Garner was wearing the dress I had seen in my dream. I knew the dream was a significant message. I wondered if she had the same dream.

She didn't have a dream as I did; Mama Garner's message came as a vision. Was she seeing angels hovering around her own daughter? By this time my mother was dealing with treatment, chemotherapy, and surgery. She seemed to leave all the healing to the doctors detaching herself from what was going on. I told Mama Garner the doctors were assured they had removed all of the cancerous cells. Mother should make a full recovery the doctors had reported. She had to strengthen her immune system to recover. This meant she had to have the mind set to restore her health. She had to have the spirit to heal.

Months went by and my mother was back to some measure of routine. She was making an effort to get involved with new friends, finding new enjoyment. It was apparent her heart wasn't in it. In spite of the prognosis she would return to full health Mama Garner and I had the same apprehensive "feeling." We didn't voice it <u>and</u> we couldn't dismiss the uneasiness we felt.

I drove the miles to the ranch to visit them. My mother was away and I found Mama Garner sitting by the window, which looked out across the yard toward the corrals. It was a sunny afternoon and she was very quiet. I hugged her and sat down to talk. As usual Mama Garner was open and candid with me as she asked, "She isn't going to make it, is she?" It wasn't really a question, but a confirmation. We were forced to face what we were sensing — clear message.

We had again felt for months the gnawing, gut feeling that my mother's sorrow was taking her life energy. She was lost without him. I answered, "No, Mama Garner, I don't think she will last more than a year."

We talked about how they had lived so close for so long that she just couldn't let it go. She didn't know how to live her life anymore. She went through the motions, but there was a certain obvious detachment. On an unconscious level her life force was waning. We both understood. Then Mama Garner began to describe her vision; it coincided with my dream. Mama Garner recalled the vivid details.

"I saw her standing out in the yard. She had on a blue dress with flowers in it. I don't know who it was, but there was a little boy with her. There were angels hovering over them. I knew I was having a vision of what was going to happen. I knew it was a vision, but I tested myself.

When she walked into the room I asked her if she had been out in the yard. Sure enough, she told me she had just returned from shopping. So I knew it was a vision. Besides, she was wearing jeans and boots, not a dress. I knew the angels were telling me she wasn't going to live. Every time I see angels hovering over someone I know they are getting ready to pass on."

We both sat quietly. The confirmation hit hard even though we both knew she was disconnecting from this life. From this point we could only support her in what she had chosen. The cancer came back and my inclination was to find new doctors and new treatments. I offered to make appointments for new methods of management and cure. She refused. Booklets and materials I brought for her to read were left unopened. I wanted to insist she try everything possible. I wanted her to fight. I had to accept this course was between her and God. I was not to judge it or interfere with it. This was a difficult lesson for me. I had to trust that Spirit was leading us. I could send light and love to her choices without interfering. I had to practice the "loving law of allowance."

Maybe it was time I listened to her angels. She and God had made an agreement. I had to support her and help only when she asked. The feeling was one of helplessness. The human part of us doesn't want to let go.

Whatever comes, we allow without judgment.

My mother asked that we have the Christmas celebration at her house that year. I wanted to convince her it would be too tiring. I wanted to say it would be easier if I had the gathering at my house. She was undergoing treatments and was becoming weaker with each day. She said this could be her last Christmas. I couldn't argue. I had to support what she was asking. Time was slipping away.

As time grew short Mama Garner and I recalled what she had seen in her vision. I reminded her the little boy beside my mother was a baby she had lost. She was in her thirties, early in the months of her pregnancy, when she miscarried. Mama Garner had forgotten about the loss.

My mother's days were spent watching the chemicals burn her veins as they exhausted any energy she had gained between treatments. From the retirement center she was moved to the hospital where her frailness incapacitated her. Her weight had dropped drastically and the treatments killed her appetite. She had no nutrition to sustain her. Her doctor's bluntness in talking about her condition was a reality that she had chosen not to face; she was overwhelmed. It seemed to drain what little strength she had. She wanted to leave the hospital. She wanted to go back to the retirement center, which was more like home, and she would be down the hallway from Mama Garner. My mother was kept out of pain while she slipped in and out of consciousness.

My mother passed in the early spring just as was shown to us. At the end I asked if she saw anyone around her, but she seemed preoccupied and unaware. I sensed she was out of her body when at one point, even through her weakness, said in a strong voice, "Someone is breathing hard in this room."

She was hearing her own breathing, but didn't recognize it. Being out of the body she was hearing it but not connecting it to the physical body in the bed. Her voice was never this strong again and she slipped into restless sleep.

She was buried in the blue dress with tiny flowers in it. Her pain was gone, and the loneliness was no more. She was where she wanted to be. Mama Garner knew she was with the angels she had seen surrounding her in the vision that day. Within the grief was the acceptance. She was teaching me again. And angels were there to help us through the sorrowful times.

Life was very different now. In these days we reminisced. Mama Garner's sharp memory had a store of tales hard to visualize in these days of paved roads, instant food, telephones, and airplanes. It was a life review and some memories were amazing.

She told about the warnings Judge Roy Bean had issued to her "Pa" when he had ridden to west Texas to round up wild Mustang horses. They drove them back to the rangeland to be trained. Their ranch house had a big welcome sign for travelers who rode on horseback migrating to new Texas territory. There was still danger of Indian raids. Mama Garner was a young wide-eyed child taking it all in. Her young life was just beginning in this new frontier land of Texas.

Mama Garner remembered the first time she met Daddy Babe — he was a quiet four year old who didn't say one word as their family came that day to introduce themselves. They had just moved onto a neighboring ranch so they saw each other from time to time in the coming days. Going to school and church together gave them time to grow up, fall in love, and create a life where her family had begun. They had seen tremendous and unbelievable changes. They watched homesteads established and towns being built. Inventions were racing. Technology was changing lifestyles rapidly. Progress was being made. They saw much in their lifetime.

Mama Garner was now 104 years old. She was still a character. She still had her sense of humor and her delightful giggle. She was still telling stories and making friends in the retirement home. There was one thing she said that I still laugh at. "A lot of the people who come to visit me just come to see what it looks like to be a hundred and four," she said. I'm sure she was right since little got past her.

Times when she would say she was getting too tired and was just going to die, I had demanded she not leave until she got to be on Willard Scott's Today program for being over a hundred. She would laugh, but she did stay with me. Willard Scott sent very thoughtful regrets that he couldn't get everyone onto the program. A record number of people live past one hundred in these times. Each year we submitted her picture, but she never got on. So maybe she kept waiting. I teased her that she would make it next year. We just weren't ready for her to go. She still had friends and enjoyed their visits.

I had moved to Dallas for a short time and then began to travel. Eventually, I spent more and more time in the Northwest traveling back and forth to Texas. With each visit she let me know she thought I was crazy for going all over the world, many times alone. I would call her and some times not tell her every place I had been. But, then she knew I was part of her, always curious.

At each visit, when she and I were alone, we would talk about her visions and dreams. Most of her visions had brought information to those close to her. This is less common. Usually, it is more difficult to read those around us since we have logical thinking to deal with. I was telling her of the work I was doing in metaphysics, and she knew I had to do it. She knew it was my purpose without realizing it was an extension of what she had done all her life. I doubt she ever realized, even though I told her, the impact she had on my life. In a reading I had long ago I was told Mama Garner was my guide in this life and would be my guide from the other side. I loved knowing this. It seemed so logical.

It was Christmas time. I made the trip from the Northwest to see her. I picked up her favorite snack of chicken livers and found her having lunch in the dining room with a few others. Her friends shared the food and then we went back to her room. We looked at new pictures someone had sent to her. We caught up on all the family news of who was doing what. She would tell me about everyone that had visited her lately, and then say she was forgetting so much these days. I reminded her that she had over a hundred years of experiences recorded in her memory bank so it was alright to forget a little. I combed her hair, and found a robe she had been looking for.

Then we talked. She told me she was getting ready to go. I had always talked her out of it, telling her we weren't through with her yet, but she would laugh. She would tell me how she was getting too tired now and was just too old. I reminded her, "You will be one hundred and five and that will be something to celebrate!" I realized I wasn't convincing her this time. This time it was different.

A sad feeling swept over me.

Then she said, “Lola is coming to sleep with me at night.”

Lola was her sister who had been gone for many years. I knew she “visited” with Daddy Babe every night, but she had never said she had been visited by any of her sisters before. It hit me hard. Was she seeing her own angels gathering? I felt she was saying goodbye. I would never be ready, but I had to acknowledge what she was telling me.

We talked and remembered good times and laughed a lot, just like we always did. I told her I had to fly to Las Vegas and was heading to the airport. She gave me her usual “Lord have mercy…you be careful.” I hugged her and we kissed each other goodbye. I told her I loved her and I would be calling her. And then, she said something I will never forget, probably the most promising words I’ve ever heard.

“You know, I don’t know whether I’m *dead* or *alive* now!” she said.”

“Well, you are talking to me in the physical, Mama Garner, but it doesn’t matter. You can talk to me on either side,” I assured her. As we hugged I wondered if I was saying goodbye to her physical being.

I have never had anything impact me the way those words did. As I headed to the airport the impact was stronger and stronger. Mama Garner was floating in and out of the physical with total ease. She could choose. She would simply walk through the veil.

This had to be the same experience people have during a near-death experience. The physical, earthbound bodies could be traumatized by injury or illness. At death they simply float out of the pain and suffering leaving the physical behind. They become the observer seeing all that is going on in the physical event. It reaffirmed, leaving the body behind does not mean death. Your energy and soul will still live on.

You go with the angels.

Her trust was without doubt. Knowing there was life after the physical death eliminated any fear of passing into that dimension. During the flight I thought about so many things she had taught me. My heart felt a surge of understanding like none I had ever encountered before. It was a joyous feeling. I smiled to think Mama Garner had given me a message straight from her angels. They were truly all around her with fluttering wings ready to go with her. I could feel her preparing, but I still didn't want to believe we were parting.

During the next few days I left Seattle going to Victoria, British Columbia in Canada spending New Year's Day in Sidney on Vancouver Island. We were waiting for the three o'clock ferry to take us to Vancouver on the mainland. We were browsing through some of the shops since we had an hour or so before the ferry left.

I couldn't believe it. There was a beautiful box of lacy linen handkerchiefs set on gold foil on one of the shelves. It was as though it had been specially boxed for Mama Garner. It was the only box nestled in the other linen items. I had to have this for her. I put it on the cashier's counter while I finished browsing. There were many people waiting for the ferry ending their holidays on the island. The day was chilly, bright and beautiful. The ferry ride was a breathtaking hour or so across the blue waters with views of the mountains along the way. Near one pass there were nests of eagles. Usually we glimpsed them gliding above the trees floating as though they were suspended. I was looking forward to sightseeing through this exceptionally beautiful country again.

Then the announcement came. Because of the holidays they had added an extra ferry so we had ten minutes to get to the terminal. We made it and drove onto the ferry minutes before two o'clock. We would be in Vancouver for the night before returning to Seattle. Then I realized I had run from the shop without buying the handkerchiefs. I was upset. I was feeling really sad since this was such a special gift. I'd never seen handkerchiefs boxed on gold foil. It was a special box.

We reached the hotel, and I checked my messages. There was a phone call with a woman's voice asking if I were there, but they left no phone number or message. I couldn't figure it out. It felt strange, but I couldn't decide why.

I arrived in Seattle the next day and began catching up on messages. I called my home in Texas. They told me Mama Garner had passed; she had been buried at two o'clock the previous day.

Even when we know, we are never ready. I was in shock. Why had no one made certain I got the message? Everyone assumed someone else had contacted me. No one had told me. I was distraught and upset. I should have been there. I couldn't understand what had happened. I mourned her physical body being gone, but another part of me was glad she was with Daddy Babe. I knew Daddy Babe met her with a hug and I'm sure she giggled. Their dog, Fluffo, was probably there wagging his white tipped tail. I knew they were smiling at each other.

I was still at a loss. Why had I not been called? How could this have happened? I had to let go. I was very confused about my feelings and why things had happened as they had. I was searching for the meaning. I had to accept that everything happens as it should, but I was feeling sad.

Then she came to me. She was reminding me and making it clear this it had been orchestrated. I wasn't supposed to be there. Maybe it was because she wasn't there. She was letting me know I was not supposed to be there for the service. That was the reason for the mix up in communication. It was the reason no one called me. Mama Garner was trying to show me she was with me. I was just feeling the grief. I asked what happened. How did she go?

Mama Garner had chosen her way and her time. She didn't go to the dining room to eat and just stayed in her bed. For the next few days she remained there. Late in the afternoon they checked on her and her breathing was becoming shallow. They told her they were going to take her to the hospital a few blocks away. She quickly informed them in her sassy way that they were to leave her alone…she threatened them if they interfered.
She continued to talk until evening then closed her eyes and passed at nine that night. She simply closed her eyes. She slept, slipping away with just one last earthly breath. Mama Garner was in the peace of the next world.

Heaven is one breath away.

The day of the burial the weather turned very cold and blustery, they told me. She was wearing the blue and white dress. Flowers draped the mound of earth. She loved lilacs and larkspurs. Her yard had been full of them with bunches of hollyhocks and climbing roses. She would probably plant a whole yard full of them in heaven, while Daddy Babe sat in the porch swing. Was she showing me where she was? Then it hit me why she didn't want me coming for the service. She wasn't there. She was with me. Mama Garner led me to the handkerchiefs to prove she was alive in a new dimension.

It was minutes before two o'clock when I was holding the handkerchiefs thinking how she would love the delicate lace that edged the white linen. The burial was taking place at that very minute and she was with me. The angels were showing me it had happened as Mama Garner had planned. She chose. I finally understood the whispers.

Angels in heaven and on earth are our guardians.

Mama Garner's spirit was strong on either side. She was busy. Daddy Babe smiled and watched. She wasn't sitting still. I sensed Mama Garner was back at one of the best times of her life in her fifties. Was what I was seeing what she 'showed' me or was that what I wanted to see? Regardless, it was assurance that she was close.

In the time following her passing I was often conscious of her being there. It felt as though she were closer now than ever. There were times I asked her to guide me and help me make decisions. It seemed she was there just for me. I was waiting for paperwork to end a legal matter. It hadn't come and I wanted it out of my life. I said aloud, "OK, Mama Garner, let them finish this up quickly so it is over and done." I received the final papers within three days. She was helping me clear everything up and my life was at last my own.

As I moved forward and things smoothed out in my life I didn't have as many requests of her. I began to feel she had moved into a different space as though she were somewhere doing research. I couldn't tell what she was doing, but she was collecting information. I knew all I had to do was ask and she'd be there to help. I even told my friends if they needed help to call on her, just get her name right — Mama Garner. She was busy, but not too busy if we needed her. She was still there to watch over me.

A friend was visiting and, of course, knew all about Mama Garner. This particular day she walked through the living room and asked, "Did Mama Garner ever say 'it's gonna come a cropper'?"

"No," I answered, thinking that didn't make sense.

Only a couple of minutes past when she questioned again, "Mama Garner never said 'it's gonna come a cropper'?"

"Oh!" I knew what it was. "She would say 'it's gonna come a whopper!"

Mama Garner always told us when it was going to storm or which day it would rain or when the first freeze would happen. So a "whopper" meant it would be a severe thunderstorm with lightning, rain, hail, and wind, "a whopper."

Within five minutes a storm hit. This area is not known for this type of thunderstorm. I heard the wind hit and raced to see what was happening. I saw a streak of lightning hit in the middle of the sound. Thunder shook the windows. Rain beat against the glass and turned quickly to pea-sized hail, which covered everything. I yelled to get away from the windows as I hurriedly unplugged electrical appliances. The strange thunderstorm hit with a fury and was gone within several minutes. It was an out-of-the-ordinary weather for the Northwest and Mama Garner had warned us.

It was a "whopper" and she had given my friend the

warning. If my friend could hear her that meant Mama Garner was with us at any time we needed her. As in life she was giving messages to help us and protect us. Was her psychic ability the key to making communication on both sides an easy exchange? When I was wondering where she was I now know she was preparing those who wanted to get messages through to this side. She was gathering information from the Akashic records. I was to discover she would bring through a vast array of people and details. Mama Garner was making the frequency connection necessary for me to hear them. It was clear I was the conduit. We were in sync.

Born under the sign of Gemini, ruler of communication, Mama Garner was still being the communicator. The purpose for the visits was to bring healing. I knew my reason was clearly laid out. I would be the message center in a sense. It was difficult to explain. I felt as though I were in a constant state of prayer. Realizing our loved ones see in detail what is going on in our every day life assures us they live on. We are learning that spirits, entities, and energies surround us continuously. It is another dimension.We sense rather than see. Being consciously aware is like gaining an extra sense, an intuitive sense.

Listen through your intuitive sense. See with other eyes.

Be guided minute-by-minute sensing the messages and signs. Our angels get our attention in various ways since we are busy human beings living in a world full of activity. Begin to notice everything.

If you find a feather: What color is it? Where did you find it? What is going on in your life?

If you find a coin: What year is it dated? Was it heads up? What denomination is it?

What does your dream symbolize? Were you were riding in a white car? Were you in a multilevel house?

Déjà vu: Did you remember a past life? Did you have a premonition of the future?

Passing thoughts: Did someone put the thoughts there? Are you getting a signal from someone?

Did the phone ring? You pick it up and realize it didn't really ring? Did you know who it was before t h e y answered? Did you dial someone who was dialing you simultaneously?

Was it your imagination? Did you really see a wisp of light? Did you smell your grandmother's bread baking? Did you hear someone call your name?

Be aware of all that is around you.
Be open to all of the messages. Ask for answers.

Ask for protection in all that you do. Find the good in every situation. Reality is what you create so make choices that are right for you…it will be right for everyone. Being good to yourself means you are being good to all energy…the people around you, the situation you are in and the universal energy.

This is getting it right!

One Whisper Away

We are one energy, connected eternally, whether in the human consciousness or in the spiritual dimension. If God is love and we are part of God then returning to pure love is the miracle we are here to create.

The why of why am I here?

It is apparent each soul chooses when to come to earth to begin the learning. Many may ignore their purpose and spend a lifetime on all of the side roads never getting on their true path. Others repeat their lessons over and over and they never get it in one lifetime. When we go through the experience, completing the lesson, we move to the next level. At this point we begin to understand *the why. Why am I here?* What are my lessons?

Wondering keeps us growing and searching. The path leads to our evolution. The understanding comes when we listen…listen with your soul…angel whispers are hushed.

The Angels whisper…blessed love…
from now until…the end...a beginning.

From the Author

Angels Whisper...they don't shout...they don't insist...they don't judge

Be still...Listen

Read and share their touching stories of the miracles that came out of contact with those on the other side. Reading about their miracles will be a shared blessing. You will see proof of detailed information passed through angels whispering to us. The inspiration you will gain by reading how they healed, forgave and found peace will give you hope and the courage to change your life. You will learn how to use your intuitive sense. In the process you will know we don't die but change dimensions. You will understand we don't lose them. They stay as near as we need them to be.

The messages are there...
from our loved ones...our guides...our angels

They speak through signs and signals...
they speak through mind words

Learn to hear through
different ears...see with different eyes.

Allow the miracles to happen in your life.

Find peace through these words

The book gives you a look at the messages, which come through from those on the other side. Death simply changes the dimension of life — it doesn't cease. The means of communication changes. Communication bridges the love between these dimensions. It heals those left behind. This book will tell you true stories of contacting the other side provoking tears and laughter and healing.

Gifts That Come From Listening

I have seen people open their minds to new possibilities and what they accepted was the transformation for their life. I know there are examples of this in the book but I saw the ripple effect within families and beyond. It brought me a better life.
Shirley Herbison, *Assistant Executive Office Administration of a northwest airplane manufacturer, Port Orchard, Washington*

Using psychic information has helped in our search for a missing young man on our reservation. Knowing that he was taken let us know, at least, that he was alive. Again, when I had to make strong boundaries with my own son, the affirmations were that I was to let him suffer the consequences of his behavior. He indeed had to pay some heavy prices but I stood firm. By my letting him learn his lessons I was able to focus on my gift of hands on healing. As results I learned I was responsible for healing myself first. Currently, I and my son are far stronger and gaining daily. The messages guided me.
Mary Hunter, *teacher and healer, Neah Bay, Washington*

For thirteen years I have received insight and understanding through readings whether it is concerning my personal life decisions or concerning career moves in my rank of military officer and government program manager. The most

important message Lou J provided was the assuredness that I was capable of developing my own ability to get answers. What I heard inspired me to live each day in fulfillment.
***R. John Primbs**, Jr., San Antonio, Texas*

I have watched the expressions and the eyes of children who were given readings during sessions. I saw the seeds start to grow in their minds recognizing their unique abilities and what their future held. The readings encouraged them to trust their own intuition.
***Marsha Murphy**, government supervisor, Federal Way, Washington*

I never cease to be amazed at the truly extraordinary details that come through the readings. You absolutely must listen. It is all about being guided in the right life direction.
***Christopher Howard**, Ph.D.(c), an internationally acclaimed Neuro Linguistic Programming expert, Manhattan Beach, California*

I recognized the importance of setting boundaries in order to have an enriched life. I learned it is walking the walk…through behavior. It is finding your spiritual path.
***George Herbison**, utility manager, Port Orchard, Washingt*on

During a reading when accurate detailed information comes through to a person it gives them a type of road map to their life. Some people give typical readings…these are not general readings…Lou J nailed it.
***Charlette LeFevre,** Coordinator, UFO Paranormal Group, Seattle, Washington*

Readings bring positive energy and taught me to look to my Higher Power bringing goodness to every corner of my life. Even when things go ‘wrong’ I look to understand the lessons that are being taught to me.
Astrid Rial*, international business owner, Lakewood, Washington*

I was skeptical at my first session but very quickly the detailed information changed my mind. It only took a minute to get details on my family, career and health condition. The suggestions for helping my allergies and sinus were on target – it worked. The method of handling my father’s death as well as dealing with my daughter, again –it worked!
P. Keller*, Port Orchard, Washington*

I have known Lou J Free since I was young and as far back as I can remember she has been like a wise spirit guide. She has, through readings and her presence, opened many doors for me that I might otherwise have never noticed. She has opened my eyes and mind to undeniable truths within the self and the universe. Every time I receive a reading or I am merely in her presence she picks up on everything going on in my life (without my ever saying a word) and opens a door allowing me to take the next step towards progress. My most recent experience with Lou opened a door that allowed me to go from unemployed to traveling the world paid for by my employer. During a reading she picked up on an contact in California and told me to make a call. The call was made and I am now in international sales, living in the San Francisco Bay Area. Since the call, I have traveled to Germany, Taiwan, Japan, Korea, Las Vegas, Italy, and

Singapore, while being paid and staying in five star hotels. Without Lou and her abilities I am sure I would have passed this opportunity up and missed seeing the world. Many thanks!!!
Joseph Witt, *international consultant, San Carlos, California*

I have to say after meeting Lou J all aspects of my life has completely changed. It started with a fifteen minute reading that lifted the weight of world off my heart. Since that first meeting she has never let go of my hand. We have a very strong soul connection. To pass on everything she has taught me I'd have to write my own book. We've learned even in hard times to look for the blessings and learn the lessons so we don't have to go there again. We know without a doubt that our loved ones on the other side are still with us. That helped us cope with the deaths of four loved ones in a very short time. It has helped all of us, me, my husband and our three daughters, to pay attention not missing any signs they give us. What a blessing. With the doors Lou J has opened I've learned how important it is to raise my girls in a spiritually open home. With much thanks and love to our dear friend, Lou J.
Sharon Thurston*, artist, Lake Tapps, Washington*

My husband told Lou J things about our life only we knew.It eased some of the pain to know he was always right there with me!
Diane James*, Honolulu, Hawaii*

About the Author

Lou J Free does private sessions for present life information, past life regression and for contacting those who have passed, your loved ones, or those who want to contact you.

If you would like to contact any of the people who have related their stories please email: **TexasWind9@aol.com**
http://www.paradisewest.com/loujfree/

Clinical Hypnotherapist
Ph.D. American Pacific University
Registered Hypnotherapist with American Board of Hypnotherapy Clinical Hypnotherapy
American Institute of Hypnotherapy
Courses Richland College,
Tarrant County Junior College
Member: International Spiritual Healers and Earth Stewards